THE
ESSENTIAL
SWIMMER

THE
ESSENTIAL
SWIMMER

STEVE TARPINIAN

ILLUSTRATED BY ROGER HUGHES

An imprint of The Globe Pequot Press

Copyright © 1996 by Steve Tarpinian
Illustrations copyright © 1996 by Roger Hughes
Published by The Globe Pequot Press
Previously published by The Lyons Press

The Lyons Press is an imprint of The Globe Pequot Press.

Design and composition by Rohani Design, Edmonds, WA

Library of Congress Cataloging-in-Publication Data

Tarpinian, Steve.
    The essential swimmer / Steve Tarpinian.
      p. cm
    Inlcudes bibliographical references and index.
    ISBN 1-55821-386-4 (pbk.)
    1. Swimming. 2. Swimming—Training. I. Title.

GV837.T37 1995
797.21—dc20   95-31776
                                                             CIP

Manufactured in the United states of America
First edition/Ninth printing

To the memory of my grandfathers:
Nishan Tarpinian and Nascenzio Russo

CONTENTS

ACKNOWLEDGMENTS

'd like to thank my oldest sister, Helen, most of all, because it was her interest in swimming that led my second sister, Marian, and then myself to the sport of swimming. And Marian, whose enthusiasm about my life and projects has always helped me weather the tough times. And my parents, Marianna and Richard, for driving me all over God's creation to swim practice (usually twice a day), and to meets (usually all weekend). They probably thought I would stop swimming at some point, but now they realize I am in it for the long haul. They both swim for fitness and my mom recently attended one of my swimming clinics!

I wish I could thank by name all the swimmers I have coached. Every one of them has contributed to my knowledge of swimming and my skills as a coach.

Special thanks to friends like Josef Mittlemann, Diane Trabulsi, and David Mayer, M.D., for helping me reach and invent some of the ideas in this book. To my triathlete buddies for always being willing to help and train with me: Ron Shuler, Steve McNight, Chris Pfund, Brian Brett, Pete Slattery, Helen Cane, Cathy Ziti, Christine Messina, Tom and Annette Macniven, Gerry Cassel, and John Lindros.

To Aaron Mattes, M.S., R.K.T., L.M.T., for his help with the chapter on flexibility; and to Tami L. Marugg, M.S., L.M.T., for her input on nutrition.

To my assistant Roger Hughes for his skills as a coach and swimmer. To John Hanc's *The Essential Runner.* To Peter Burford and my insightful editor Amy Young for seeing and sharing my vision of this book.

Lastly, to one of the most instrumental coaches in swimming, Dave Ferris. Dave coached me through all of my fastest times and showed me what I knew to be a truth: "Swimming is a thinking man's sport." Thanks, Dave.

PREFACE

This book is designed for fitness swimmers and competitors alike. It is a product of my frustration as a coach over not being able to recommend one, simple book that explains in clear terms the principles behind swim improvement.

There are two essential parts to a successful swimming program—technique and training. I will address technique first because it is the foundation. Starting to train before addressing technique is not a good idea. It is putting the cart before the horse: Any flaws you have will become ingrained as you train. You may see some improvement with premature training, but at the end of the day you will find yourself still limited by your technique. Also, no matter how advanced your swimming technique is, improvement is always a possibility—in many cases a necessity if you want to get that competitive edge and avoid injury. Through practical technique coaching and step-by-step illustrations, this book will enable you to make stroke corrections and get the edge you are looking for.

Once you have secured good technique, appropriate workouts become exponentially more effective. These workouts will combine stroke drills, kicking drills, and interval sets, which together will make your training more effective and fun. In addition to technique and training, *The Essential Swimmer* will address many other swimming-related topics such as swimming aids, open-water and competitive swimming, flexibility, strength training, nutrition, and cross training.

■ ■ ■

My swimming background began over 20 years ago, at a time when I was deathly afraid of the water. My dad tells the story best. I was about five years old and the family was at Lake Champlain. I stood at the water's edge frightened even to touch it because of the "waves." These waves were two- to three-inch ripples! Luckily for me, my parents and sisters were supportive; within a few years I became comfortable in the water. Since then I have always maintained my respect for it. As an ocean lifeguard I have had many opportunities to see the power of water and to realize that a little fear and caution—viewed in a positive way—will enhance the swimming experience. My grandfather was a man of few words, but he had some poignant morsels about what to be careful of. He said, "Always respect water, fire, and steam."

I have had many terrific coaches, read many books, and studied many videos, and now I will share the most effective swimming strategies with you. Have confidence in my plan for you: These principles and workouts have been proven effective by the success of our swimmers at the Total Training Swim Clinics, and by the people who have successfully used our video, *Swim Power*, to improve both their enjoyment of and their performance in the water. You and I share two things: an interest in swimming and the desire to improve. Thanks for joining me; I am honored that you have chosen me as your coach.

1

SWIMMING

HISTORY

You may think of swimming as a less natural human skill than walking or running, but in actuality swimming dates farther back in our evolution than walking. Because we evolved from fish (did you know human embryos still have gills?), we have great potential for being comfortable in the water. If the aquatic environment seems foreign to you, remember where you came from and have some faith. If fear of the water is a concern for you, then I suggest you start very slowly—perhaps even by simply remaining in the shallow end of the pool for your first swim session. Anything to start to relax in the water. A good community swimming class with other people is usually helpful. Just make sure the instructor is sensitive to your fears.

The earliest real proof that man (the mammal) is a swimmer comes from cave drawings dating back to 9,000 B.C. that have been unearthed in the Middle East. These drawings depict people swimming something that resembles the breaststroke. In ancient Greece and Rome swimming was a standard part of military training.

Pools were not made specifically for swim competitions until the 1908 Olympic Games in London. Up until then swimming was mostly a leisure activity; breaststroke, sidestroke, and backstroke were used. Some races—mostly sidestroke—were conducted in open-water areas, such as harbors. At a sidestroke race in the late 1800s, much to the surprise and shock of the competitors and officials, one swimmer started taking one arm out of the water while performing sidestroke. Since there were no rules saying you could not take your arm out of the water, this innovative swimmer won easily, creating a new stroke called the "trudgen" (named after J. Trudgen, the English swimmer who introduced it, incorrectly copying it from a Native American style). One kick for each arm stroke was called the single trudgen; two kicks for each stroke was called the double trudgen. This set the precedent for further innovations in swimming. Eventually the trudgen dropped the froglike (breaststroke/sidestroke) kick in favor of the flutter kick, and came to use both arms alternating. This new stroke was popularized by the Australians and was called the "Australian crawl."

The event called "freestyle" allows you to swim any style (free-style) you wish. Since Australian crawl is the fastest way to go, *freestyle* and *crawl* have become synonymous. For purposes of consistency I will refer to the crawl as "freestyle" throughout this book. For both competition and fitness, freestyle is today the most popular and widely used stroke. That is why this book focuses primarily on it.

You can see that from the beginning of swimming's history, it has been a fast-changing sport. One very interesting innovation in freestyle came when a swimmer performed a flip turn in competition. The rules at that time stated you had to touch the wall with your hand to turn. He simply brushed his hand on the wall and flipped. Eventually the rules were changed to allow for a no-hand (feet only) touch. This change made freestyle records faster, because of the time saved by using flip turns over "open" turns (more on this in chapter 2). Changes are taking place most recently in the "off-strokes"—strokes other than freestyle. Although some leisure swimmers still use sidestroke and elementary backstroke, there are only four recognized strokes for competition: freestyle, backstroke, breaststroke, and butterfly. Butterfly used to be performed with a breaststroke kick. Then a swimmer did it with the dolphin kick; this changed the whole stroke, making it faster. Then there was a backstroker in the '80s who realized he could increase his speed by swimming the entire first lap underwater (kicking only). These are the kinds of innovations that make swimming so exciting and ever changing.

Many developments in technology have enhanced swimming's development. Underwater cameras have helped coaches dissect exactly what the better swimmers do to make them so fast. Goggles allow you to stay in the water longer and see the walls better when turning. Electronic timing has made for more accurate finishing order and times when determining records.

Recently I had the opportunity to meet Dr. Marty Hull in California. Marty is at the leading edge in the development of swimming products that benefit swimmers. His Zoomers™ Fins have been used by many with incredible results. His latest invention, The Towing Machine, will no doubt revolutionize swim training. This machine tows you down the pool by way of a cable so you can experience swimming at speeds faster than you can currently attain. This experience gives you and your coach information invaluable to making the changes necessary to swim faster.

It is interesting to note that many swimmers are heading back to the open water to swim. Whether for training or racing or just plain recreation, open water contains an element of adventure you cannot find in the pool. You will never have a problem finding an "open lane" at the beach. There are other factors to consider in open water, however, such as boats, jet skis, surfers, and creatures. Swimming in protected (lifeguard-on-duty) areas is your smartest option. Triathlon is a growing sport and one of its key appeals is the sense of adventure and survival gained by swimming in the open water.

Whether in the open water or a backyard pool, during an athlete's off-season or year-round, there are estimated to be over 63 million active swimmers in the United States. This explains why on any ranking of sports' participation levels, swimming is always right at the top.

SWIMMING BENEFITS

Why is swimming so terrific? It is a cardiovascular work-out that uses many, if not all, of the body's muscles. In addition to its prime movers—latissimus dorsi, deltoids, biceps, triceps, chest, quadriceps, hamstrings, abdominals, and back—swimming employs virtually all your muscles in a synergistic way. This brings fresh blood and nutrients to all areas of your body, creating a total-body-flushing effect that removes dangerous toxins and helps rejuvenate virtually every body tissue. Swimming also helps build your body in a proportioned way—for the Tarzan in you. Other sports can give you bulky, awkward, and dispropor-tioned muscles; the swimmer's build is not only practical but aesthetically pleasing.

Unlike running or jogging, swimming is practically injury-free. No pounding of the body takes place—all of its movements are cushioned by water. Many people, includ-ing world class athletes, have used the healing properties of water to successfully recover from injuries. This is one of the most important reasons why so many people are involved in swimming. It is truly an activity for all ages and abilities—infants, children, teens, adults, senior citizens, the elderly, pregnant women, the physically challenged, injured people, and arthritis patients can all participate in this sport. Trainers, therapists, coaches, and doctors have been prescribing water activity more and more.

The watery environment is also very conducive to relaxation and stress relief. You can use your swimming session to escape or focus—depending on what is going on for you personally. Many swimmers find a good long swim helps them handle life's challenges. Ever try tuning out of reality while jogging down Fifth Avenue? When you swim, there is no sound except the water sliding around your head. Personally, I find that my whole outlook can change after a swim workout. Many times I have gone to the pool dreading my session thinking "This is not what I need"; but I have never left the pool without feeling better for having gone. Squeezing in a swim, no matter how short, is always worthwhile.

Since most pools are maintained at between 70 and 80 degrees F (21 and 25 degrees C) their temperature gives a little shock to the body (which operates at 98.6 F—35.3 C), but that is just one of the reasons you usually do not lie around in a pool—you move. You swim, kick, jump—anything to get the blood circulating. This stimulation, while at first uncomfortable, should be viewed as one of the wonderful benefits of swimming. We all need a little jump start sometimes.

Swimming can also be either a social or a solitary endeavor. Joining a masters team can instantly bond you with a group of comrades. Swimmers have unique ties—in how many other sports do participants shave their entire bodies for competitions? Sharing a pizza after a tough practice and questioning the sanity of your coach is always a good time. Going to swim meets affords you the opportunity to meet new people and exchange ideas on training, work, family, and life. On the flip side, not all sports can offer the meditative and solitary pleasures that swimming can. As great as all that comradery stuff is, you can always go off into an end lane and be in your own world. Swimming is a sport that truly does offer the best of both worlds.

Other than the problem of locating a pool that is available at the right time for you, swimming is pretty much a hassle-free, no-strings activity. Pools are common in cities and towns via clubs, Ys, and schools. A suit, some goggles, and maybe a cap is the extent of the equipment that you will need.

To sum it all up, swimming is a great cardiovascular workout that is practically injury-free, with great stress-relieving and jump-start potential, to be enjoyed with comrades or in quiet solitude, exciting to watch (especially college dual meets and triathlons) and even more exciting to compete in (especially when it includes the adventure of open water).

2

FREESTYLE
TECHNIQUE

In real estate the three keys are 1) location, 2) location, and 3) location; in swimming the three keys are 1) technique, 2) technique, and 3) technique.

This chapter is devoted to freestyle technique because, as I mentioned in chapter 1, freestyle is the most widely used of the four major swimming strokes. Not only is it the fastest and in many ways the easiest stroke, but many principles of its technique can also be applied to the other strokes. For example, backstroke can be viewed as freestyle performed on your back. The kick used in backstroke is the same used in freestyle, with a slight change in the ratio of force exerted by the fronts and backs of your thighs. Butterfly, too, is similar to freestyle in that you perform the same pull patterns with your arms, although both arm cycles occur simultaneously in butterfly rather than alternating as in freestyle. Breaststroke diverges the most from freestyle, but still includes some aspects of the freestyle pull. All strokes use the streamlined body position, the exhale while your face is in the water (except for backstroke), and that elusive "feel for the water." Chapter 5 will provide a reference guide for understanding the basics of these other strokes.

There are many books on freestyle technique and many different theories. Even when watching the Olympics you will see many variations in technique—even some that might be labeled "poor." I mention this hoping you will

---

THE SIX ASPECTS*
OF FREESTYLE TECHNIQUE

---

1. Arm cycle	each cycle consists of five phases: entry, elbow flexion (catch), pull (adduction), release (and round-off), and recovery
2. Rotation	long axis rotation and shoulder rotation
3. Body position	staying streamlined to reduce drag
4. Kicking	important in maintaining proper body position
5. Breathing	a result of proper rotation
6. Push off	sets the stage for the lap

* Note: I will discuss these six aspects of freestyle technique one at a time and explain how to perform each one properly. However, it is important to realize that, when swimming, all are being performed in a continuous cycles.

keep in mind that we are all individuals who need to find our own best techniques. To do this, however, a knowledge of basic freestyle technique is essential.

Besides enabling you to swim faster and more efficiently, good technique greatly reduces your chances of sustaining a shoulder injury. Shoulder injury, usually in the form of tendonitis, is the most prevalent swimming injury. With proper technique it is completely avoidable, making swimming, as I mentioned earlier, one of the least injury-prone sports. This chapter contains clear explanations of the basics of freestyle technique, beginning with a distillation of its six most important aspects: arm cycle, rotation, body position, kicking, breathing, and the push-off. Turns are addressed at the end of the chapter, and advanced freestyle technique is explored in the following chapter.

ARM CYCLE

The arm cycle can be broken down into five phases: entry, elbow flexion (catch), pull (adduction), release (and round-off), and recovery. Since freestyle uses a continuous arm cycle, there is no first or last phase. None of these phases is isolated. If one phase is performed incorrectly then the entire stroke suffers! In swimming, as in many sports, you are only as strong as your weakest link.

PHASE 1 – ENTRY

Entry occurs when you slip your hand into the water and extend your arm forward. Your goal is to enter as smoothly as possible and really extend your arm forward to prepare for the next stage, elbow flexion.

During entry, slip your hand into the water 8 to 12 inches (20 to 30 cm) in front of your shoulder, making

Hand entry (phase 1)

approximately a 45-degree angle with the water's surface. Once your hand is in the water, extend your arm forward. This extension comes from rotating your body, extending your arm, and elevating your shoulder. As your hand extends forward, rotate your arm toward your midline so that your palm becomes parallel with the bottom of the pool.

Extension and medial rotation (phase 1)

As you extend your arm, think of sliding your hand forward just under the surface of the water. This will create lift. Often swimmers dive or drive the hand down. This action causes two problems: First, you get little or no lift, and second, you get into a poor position for the next phase, thereby compromising power.

PHASE 2 – ELBOW FLEXION (CATCH)

Elbow flexion is a bending of your elbow underwater after the entry phase. Its purpose is to create a large pulling surface for the pull phase that follows. If you perform little or no elbow flexion then your only pulling surface is your hand. With proper elbow flexion, your hand and forearm become one large paddle.

Elbow flexion picks up where the entry ends, with your arm fully extended and your hand parallel to the bottom of the pool. You then bend your elbow to a 90-degree angle.

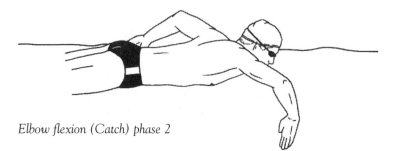

Elbow flexion (Catch) phase 2

Your wrist can bend slightly to initiate the bending of your elbow—just be sure to straighten it after your elbow is fully bent. This is not a powerful movement, but it is a movement that sets up the stroke and should not be rushed.

Catch is a mere descriptive term for this movement that has you bending your elbow and rotating your shoulder at the same time. *Note:* You must turn the shoulder in as you bend the elbow. This is what sweeps the hand out and gets you in the position (see illustration). Take your time learning elbow flexion—it will pay big dividends. It sets the stage for the power phase, the pull (or adduction). The importance of elbow flexion is an agreed-upon fact among coaches. Swimmers can sacrifice other aspects of technique and still be great, but a great swimmer cannot get away with poor elbow flexion—in any of the four strokes. So if you learn anything, learn to avoid the common error of dropping your elbow and pulling with only your hand. Keep your elbow raised, bend it, and make powerful use of your entire forearm.

PHASE 3 – PULL (ADDUCTION)

The pull or adduction is the power phase of the stroke. It is an accelerating movement and causes the majority of your forward propulsion. Literally, adduction is the move‑ment of a limb toward the midline of your body. In this case I actually mean along your midline.

To pull you should—while keeping your elbow bent and using your forearm and hand as one large paddle—depress your shoulder and employ your back muscles to bring your arm and hand past your swimsuit. As your hand passes your chest, use your tricep muscles to extend your arm (elbow straight) for the finish of the pull phase.

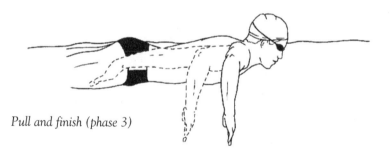

Pull and finish (phase 3)

Although your hand should pull through an S‑shaped pull pattern, to find "still" water for greater resistance, you do not need to consciously do this. Good long axis rota‑tion will cause this S‑pattern. (I have found that consciously working on an S‑pattern distracts all begin‑ning, all intermediate, and some advanced swimmers. Your effort and time are much better spent working on rotation—see this chapter's next section.) Be careful not to pull your arm too far under your body. Underwater video footage is very helpful for analyzing this phase.

PHASE 4 - RELEASE (AND ROUND-OFF)

The release is the phase in which, once you have finished your pull and your arm can extend back no further, the

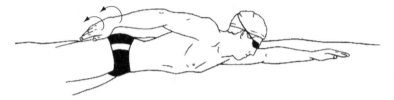

Release and round off (phase 4)

arm relaxes for a clean exit, and the shoulder joint opens so that you can take a smooth and injury free recovery.

After finishing your pull (adduction), your palm should be turned in slightly so that it is facing your leg. This is your hand's natural position, and it allows for a relaxed, clean exit, led by your pinkie. Once your hand has exited, turn out your palm slightly—as though you are throwing a ball. This turning-out of your hand is crucial to releasing your shoulder joint and preventing unnecessary strain on your shoulder.

If the release movement seems awkward, try practicing with a ball or a tennis racket. Go through the motions of either throwing or hitting the ball. Notice how you turn out your hand on the wind-up. That turning-out comes from externally rotating your shoulder. This opens your shoulder joint, allowing smooth recovery. Although this is a small movement, do not minimize its importance. Not releasing can cause irreparable damage to your shoulder. Usually the pain comes after the damage, so always make sure you are releasing correctly.

PHASE 5 - RECOVERY

Recovery is the bringing forward of your arm above the water. It is the link between the finish of the pull, and the entry.

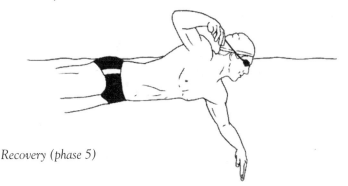

Recovery (phase 5)

After the release, relax your hand and concentrate on bringing your elbow forward. As your elbow reaches your shoulder area, your forearm and hand come forward, ready to enter the water again. Try to relax your arm as much as possible.

Keep in mind that this is the only phase in which your arm gets a chance to rest. Sometimes it helps to think of the recovery as a reaction to the rest of the stroke—similar to a rubber band being stretched, then released. Be sure you do not have too much tension in your arm during the recovery. Play around with flopping your arm forward. This will help relax your arm.

ROTATION

At the same time that your arms are cycling through the five phases of the arm cycle, two types of rotation are taking place—long axis rotation and shoulder rotation. This is where many swimmers have problems; they do not rotate and, as you will see, they rob themselves of longer

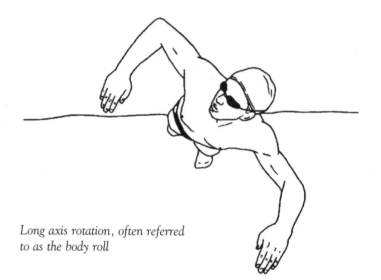

Long axis rotation, often referred to as the body roll

and more powerful strokes. Long axis rotation (sometimes referred to as a "body roll") is a rotation of your entire body. Imagine a string attached to your spine and coming straight up through the top of your head. This string is your long axis. When rotating correctly, your entire body rotates back and forth along this axis in a segmented fashion: shoulders and chest, followed by torso, hips, and, finally, legs. This long axis rotation enables you to take longer and more powerful strokes by enabling you to reach out farther and gain power from your hips—as essential in good swimming as it is in other sports such as baseball, golf, boxing, and tennis. When good long axis rotation is present, you can almost feel the pull being initiated by your hips and legs.

Some swimmers swim flat, with no rotation, and therefore have weak, short strokes. A more common problem—among inexperienced and advanced swimmers alike—is rotating the upper body and not the lower body. This creates extra drag and is referred to as "fishtailing." As the nonrotating hips come out of the slipstream they create drag and slow you down. In some cases lower back inflexibility can add to the problem. However, as you will see in chapter 9, flexibility can be increased.

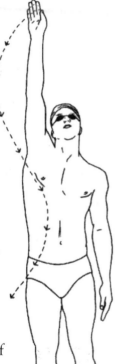

Although it is possible to overrotate (long axis), I have never seen this problem. As a matter of fact, I frequently ask swimmers to overrotate (even flip over) to really feel the rotation along their entire bodies.

Strokes are more powerful when combined with good long axis rotation, in part because of the effects of sculling. Sculling is the act of moving a limb back and forth to create force at a 90-degree angle to the movement. There

S-pull pattern

is no question that swimmers scull. However, the important and practical question is: How do they do it? This sculling motion is sometimes referred to as the "S-pattern pull," because your hand moves through an S-pattern (as viewed from the bottom of the pool). This outward-inward-outward sweep movement is confusing and next to impossible to teach beginner and intermediate swimmers. As I mentioned before, I prefer to not have swimmers think of sculling as a separate aspect of swimming. In freestyle and backstroke, sculling occurs naturally during the pull, if good body rotation along the long axis is present.

The other type of rotation which takes place simultaneously with the long axis rotation or body roll, is the rotation of your shoulders: Your shoulders rotate, in an oval or forward-shrug-type movement, with the stroke. During recovery your shoulder goes up and forward (biomechanically it is elevating); during the pull your shoulder goes down and backward (biomechanically it is depressed). This "rotation," if performed correctly, allows you to get four to eight inches (10 to 20 cm) more from each stroke. Doing some standing, forward shoulder shrugs with a light (5 lb or 2 kg) dumbbell will help give you the feeling of shoulder rotation.

Shoulder rotation

Rotation is a crucial aspect of swimming: It is the basis for smooth breathing, long strokes, and power.

BODY POSITION

When swimming freestyle your body should ride almost horizontally in the water, with a slight upward angle. Your head should be positioned so that the waterline is between your goggles and your hairline. Your shoulders should ride along the surface of the water, while your feet should be 3 to 6 inches (8 to 15 cm) below the surface. This is the highest sustainable body position.

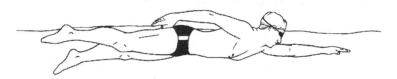

Correct body position

Correct body position is very important because it helps minimize drag. Some people find the comparison of aerodynamics to aquadynamics helpful in understanding streamlining (minimizing drag). Just as sticking your hand out the window of an automobile places it under intense pressure, so shooting your leg out of the slipstream slows you down. You have no choice but to go out of the slipstream to pull and kick; minimizing unnecessary motion, however, will increase the efficiency of your stroke.

Correct body position is a natural fallout of working on the other aspects of freestyle technique. It is an area on which you do not need to concentrate too much. Having a strong lower back and abdomen will help you keep a good high body position. Visualizing is also very helpful. Watch swimmers with good position either live or, better yet, on tape. Many swimmers benefit, too, from closing their eyes, visualizing the position described above, and thinking of a speedboat that has planed off. Focusing on the pressure on your chest is another way to help get the feel of it.

The two areas on which you can concentrate on are your feet and your head. Where you kick—in terms of depth—will have a profound effect on your body position. If your feet come too far out of the water, your head and upper body will be forced down. Conversely, if your kick is very deep, much of your energy is diverted into keeping your body up and overcoming the additional drag caused by coming so far out of the slipstream. Ideally, kick just below the surface (see the kicking section in this chapter). At the other end of your body, your head is also part of the body-position equation. Where you focus your eyes dictates your body position. When your head is in the proper position you will be looking 3 to 4 feet (1 to 1 ¼ m) in front of you, at either the bottom of the pool or the wall. Many swimmers make the mistake of looking directly down. This will force your head down and lower your position. Generally a good head position and steady kick lead the way.

KICKING

Almost all of your forward movement in swimming comes from your upper body, during the pull or adduction phase of the arm cycle. Only in sprinting do you gain any appreciable forward propulsion from kicking. Instead, kicking is very important in setting up the best environment for maximizing your strength—namely, by securing rhythm, stability, and good body position.

Freestyle flutter kick

The kick in freestyle, referred to as the "flutter kick," consists of two movements: an upbeat and a downbeat. These two movements are performed in opposition to each other. In other words, when one leg is working on an upbeat, the other is performing a downbeat. Also, the majority of this flutter kick takes place underwater, but no more than 6 to 8 inches (15 to 20 cm) deep.

The kicking movement needs to be initiated from the large muscles of your buttocks and upper leg. One way to simulate this is to lie on your back and lift your legs off the ground as though you were doing a leg lift. When your legs are 6 to 12 inches (15 to 30 cm) off the ground, try the flutter kick in the air, keeping your legs straight and toes pointed. This is tough on your abdominals, so go easy. Knee flexion is needed only at the very end of the kick, and even then it is slight. One of the keys to a successful flutter kick is to relax your lower legs—this provides a whip effect at the end of the kick. From the outside the flutter kick looks like boiling water—the heels just popping out of the water slightly. The most effective kick is a small one. If the kick is too large, it will come too far out of the slipstream and create unwanted drag.

The freestyle kick helps you keep a nice rhythm by the dynamics of using limbs in opposition. Just as your arms help you maintain pace and rhythm while you walk or run, the legs help you maintain your pace and rhythm while you swim. This opposing-limb scenario also helps stabilize your body. Imagine how unstable running would be with your hands at your sides! The body was designed to be used in opposition. Dancers sometimes use a walk called the "robot"—the right arm and right leg are moved at the same time, then the left arm and left leg. Try this and feel how unnatural it is, and why they call it the "robot." Finally, a good kick enhances body position by keeping your upper body high, and keeping your legs from dragging like anchors. The key to a good kick is to keep it in the slipstream as much as possible. To sprint, kick faster, not bigger.

There are three basic kick patterns: 2-beat, 4-beat, and 6-beat. The number of beats for a kick pattern is the number that occur during two complete arm cycles. The 2-beat is the most widely used pattern. In the 2-beat, kick once for each stroke, in opposition. (The 2-beat is the only pattern in which the opposition is one-to-one.) This pattern provides rhythm and a good body position; but not much forward propulsion. The 4-beat has two kicks to every stroke, and provides a little more propulsion. The 6-beat kick is usually used for sprinting; it cannot be maintained for long distances. There is less rotation in the 4- and 6-beat kicks than in the 2-beat. In general sprinting is an inefficient way to swim, which is one of the reasons it cannot be maintained for long.

BREATHING

Proper breathing occurs as part of your long axis rotation. As your body rotates to the side, you should need to turn your head only slightly to get a comfortable breath. Notice where your eyes are focused when you breathe. Your gaze should be about 5 degrees forward of an imaginary line emerging at a 90-degree angle from your head.

Always exhale fully, with your face in the water, before breathing. Do not hold your breath. The first lesson I teach children in swim classes is to blow bubbles

Proper breathing for freestyle

with their faces in the water. If you find you are holding your breath, try the bubble-blowing drill. Stand in the shallow end of the pool and bend forward at your waist. With one hand on the edge of the pool, place your face in the water. Exhale fully, then turn your head and shoulders (to simulate the feeling of long axis rotation) to the side to inhale. It is never too late to learn the right way. Breathing should also be as relaxed as possible, with smooth inhalation and smooth exhalation. Short, quick breaths will certainly put you into oxygen debt way before your time. Often frustrated swimmers describe breathing in freestyle with words like: *choking, panting, drowning,* or *dying.* In all of these cases the angst can be attributed to a staccato breathing pattern. Fixing this may well be the key to enjoying swimming. It cannot be fixed overnight, but most people can fix it quickly, because identifying it as the problem is 90 percent of the battle. Make your breathing as natural as possible and utilize the bubble-blowing drill as much as necessary.

Breathing patterns in freestyle are broken into two categories: single-sided breathing and bilateral breathing. "Single-sided" breathing means always turning to breathe on the same side. "Bilateral" means turning alternately to the right, and then to the left, for a breath. If bilateral (alternate-side) breathing is a stumbling block, then master single-sided breathing first. (And always race or perform fast sets with whichever type of breathing feels most comfortable.) Once you are ready, though, there are definite technique advantages to bilateral breathing: It helps you even out your stroke and rotate evenly on both your sides. You should therefore try to use it as often as possible. The bilateral pattern can be done in odd numbers of strokes: 3, 5, 7, and so on. Single-sided breathing can be done in even numbers of strokes: 2, 4, 6, and so on.

Hypoxic training is the technique of depriving yourself of oxygen by breathing less. I personally have not found much benefit from it, with the exception of sprint training. A common set to do when practicing hypoxic training is to increase the number of strokes you take without breathing by 2 every lap for 4 laps, then repeat the pattern. Use caution when practicing hypoxic training, as you may feel faint. And unless you plan on doing a sprint race, you should skip the technique.

PUSH-OFF

A push-off is the beginning of each lap and your opportunity to get your speed going. You perform a push-off to start a swim; it is also a part of every turn, whether an open turn or a flip turn.

Too many swimmers (especially triathletes, open-water swimmers, and fitness swimmers) feel they do not need to work on the push-off because it makes swimming easier. The fact is, you cannot swim as fast as a good push-off. Good push-offs, therefore, help keep you going fast, and that is the best training you can do.

ANATOMY OF A GOOD PUSH-OFF

Hold on to the wall of the pool with one hand, keeping one foot against the wall. Pull yourself toward the wall and bring up your bottom foot so that your feet are 6 to 8 inches (15 to 20 cm) apart. With a "push," straighten your legs, rotate onto your stomach as you come off the wall, and stretch into your streamline. (Visualizing a corkscrew can be helpful.) Put one hand on top of the other and squeeze your arms onto your ears. Your body will naturally rise. As you come to the surface, start your pull to initiate swimming. This first stroke is referred to as the "breakout stroke."

TURNS

There are two ways to turn at the wall in freestyle: the open turn and the flip turn. The open turn is when you come into the wall, touching it with either one or both

A push off consists of: starting on the wall. . .

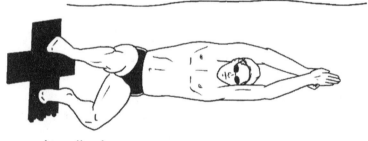

. . . pushing off underwater. . .

. . . and streamlining.

hands, then pull your body into the wall and push off. The flip turn is accomplished by following your last stroke into the wall with a flip and pushing off the wall with your feet. In a flip turn your hand never touches the wall. For many swimmers flip turns epitomize finesse and skill.

As a swim coach I am often asked, "Should I do flip turns?" While flip turns are not requisite for a good training program, they can really make a big difference in your swimming. Flip turns are not for competitive pool swimmers only. Fitness swimmers, triathletes, and open-water swimmers derive great benefit from training with flip turns. Flip turns allow you to maintain swimming continuity, as opposed to open turns, which require you to stop at every lap. In addition, being able to do flip turns is usually an indication of having "arrived" as a swimmer. Anyone who does open turns knows how frustrating it is to swim faster than the swimmer in the next lane, but watch the slower swimmer flip at the turn and thus gain a body-length lead. Learning to perform flip turns properly is a challenge, and can be very rewarding.

There are three phases to a flip turn: the approach, the flip, and the push-off. The best way to learn the flip turn is to master one phase at a time.

The first phase, the approach, is the easiest phase. It will take you some time to learn to gauge where you should take your last stroke—this spot varies from individual to individual and from pool to pool, depending on your height, speed, and so on, and gauging it can only be mastered through trial-and-error practice. Start by flipping a little too far from the wall, and with each attempt get a little closer. Most pools have crosses on the bottom and on

A *flip turn consists of: approaching the wall. . .*

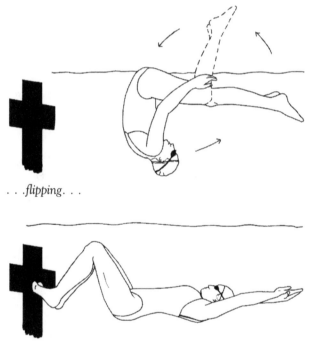

. . .*flipping.* . .

. . .*pushing off on one's back* . . .

the wall; try to not get too used to these markings, though, because they vary from pool to pool. What you should really focus on is the wall itself. If you have a good head

. . .rotating onto one's side while pushing off. . .

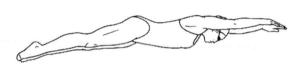

. . .and finally rotating onto one's stomach.

position your eyes will be focused about 3 to 4 feet (1 to 1
¼ m) in front of your head. That is just about the right distance to start tucking your head. As you can see, you need
to anticipate your last stroke. When it is finished and both
hands are at your sides, you are ready for the flip.

The middle phase, the flip itself, is actually a somersault performed while moving forward. This is the phase
that most people have trouble with. If this movement is
hard for you to master, you can practice by performing
somersaults in the water from a standing position. I also
suggest watching children performing it—children love
doing somersaults in the middle of the pool. It is at this
point that I get into the water myself to help swimmers
tuck their heads and get their legs over. When you actually do a flip turn you will open up your legs more than
when you practice a somersault—your feet should be a
shoulder width apart as they come over your body. You

should also pike your body by bending at the waist at an angle of 90 degrees.

For the final phase, push off while on your back and, as you come off the wall underwater, roll over onto your stomach. Remember to streamline as you push off so that you can carry some good speed into the next lap. This is referred to as the "flat" flip turn. (Another, less efficient type of flip involves rotating onto your stomach as you flip.) As the name implies, you push off while flat on your back. Remember to breathe out during the push-off.

Flip turns can be very stressful for swimmers; many fear cracking their heels on the wall, running out of air, or getting water up their noses. Flip turns are not mandatory. Take the pressure off yourself. If you fear hitting the wall, realize that when swimmers misjudge the wall it is usually because they flip too early and "miss" it. Running out of air or getting water up your nose are due to problems with your exhalation. If you get water up your nose, you are not breathing out. Possibly you breathed out too fast; possibly you did not breathe out enough. If you run out of air, you let your air out too fast. The trick to smooth flip turns is to take a deep breath as you approach the wall, then exhale slowly and steadily as you flip.

One of the great things about flip turns is that you can adjust them on the fly. If you end up too close to the wall you can just ball up. If you end up too far away, you can open up your legs a bit and allow your momentum to carry you to the wall.

The last thing to note about flip turns is practice. Your first flips will not be pretty. Go for it anyway. Commit to a finite number of turns per workout; increase this number every week, until you are performing flips on all your turns. Missing a turn is common, even for experienced swimmers, so do not allow that to discourage you.

■ ■ ■

I can hear you saying, "How can I possibly keep track of all these technical, coordinated movements—head position, entry, elbow flexion, kicking, recovery, pull, breathing, and so on?" You cannot (at least not all at the same time). When freestyle is performed correctly it is with little or no conscious thought. I like to compare it to swinging a golf club. When you really connect with one it is as though it just happened. All your lessons and effort finally show up when you let go. The best way to work on your technique, therefore, is to practice it one aspect or phase at a time. Chances are you have mastered many aspects of good technique already. The next chapter will help you pinpoint exactly what to correct and how.

3

PERFECTING
YOUR FREESTYLE
TECHNIQUE

Limited technique yields limited potential,
Improving technique equals unlimited potential.

It would be impossible to teach you in one chapter how to analyze your stroke. What I am out to accomplish here is to describe for you the most common stroke flaws, and to give you prescriptions for correcting them—putting more emphasis on swimming efficiently than on pounding out the laps. Since you have picked up this book and read this far I know you are serious about improving your swimming. You need, then, to perform the prescribed drills—while concentrating on your particular flaw(s). Simply doing the drills is not enough.

The best way to approach working on your technique is to start with videotaping. In swimming, unlike running and other aerobic sports, you cannot see yourself as you move. I have found in my clinics that it is virtually impossible to correct errors in swimmers' strokes if they cannot see the errors themselves. A corrective visualization process takes place when you see yourself swim. Even if you work with an excellent coach, there is too much room for error in communication to not use videotape as a tool. If you are self-conscious or afraid to see yourself, remember: "The worse it looks, the better your potential for improvement."

While underwater shots are helpful, many errors can be seen from surface video. If a coach is not available, ask a friend or lifeguard to video your swimming from different angles. Get footage of slow, medium, and fast swimming to see the differences in your stroke. Get a good clip of your push-off. Be sure the cameraperson includes front, back, side, and top (from a diving board or starting block) views of your swimming. Once you have this video, improvement is simply a matter of picking out your errors and applying the appropriate corrective drills. Analysis of this tape will hold the keys to better swimming. Videotape every two to four weeks to ensure progress.

If viewing the videotape shows you that dropping your elbow seems to be the biggest flaw in your stroke, then that should be your only focus during your stroke drills. Work on that until you either correct it, get frustrated, or make progress. The only way to really know if you are making headway is to get a video update. When you feel ready, you can begin working on another aspect of your stroke. Sometimes it helps to take a break from a tough change and get back to it at a later workout.

What follows are the most common symptoms of poor freestyle technique that I see at my swim clinics, and their corrective prescriptions (Rx). These Rx's are in the form of prescribed drills. (All of the drills are fully explained and illustrated in the next chapter.) Please remember that you must visualize the change you want to effect as you perform these drills. Performing the drills mindlessly will give you little change in your stroke.

SYMPTOM: poor push-off

A push-off can be poor for many reasons—most having to do with little or no streamlining. Here are some sure signs that you are performing a poor push-off:

1. After pushing off, you feel like you are starting to swim from a standstill.

2. Swimmers in adjacent lanes gain a significant distance on you at every turn.

3. You have no glide.

4. You push off on the surface.

The most common flaw is the "Superman push-off"— easy to recognize because the swimmer looks just like Superman, with arms apart and head up. This creates tremendous drag and forces you to start swimming from a standstill. Whether you do the Superman push-off or some variation, the following prescribed drill will help you achieve maximum streamline.

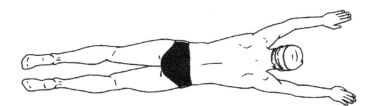

Avoid a non-streamlined push off: maybe it works for Superman, but it is not the best for swimmers.

Rx: Perform 3 to 5 push-offs, working on your streamlining and trying to travel farther with each one. Really play with the feel of the water and the angle at which you come off the wall. Experiment a little. Try arching your back more, then try a little less. See what works best. Whatever allows you to travel farther off the wall is best. Keeping a record of where you come up will help you improve.

SYMPTOM: hands crossing the midline

This is a flaw with your hand entry. Your hand entry should be 8 to 12 inches (20 to 30 cm) in front of your shoulder, and should extend directly in front of your shoulder—even slightly outside. Your arm extends with the help of long axis rotation.

Avoid having your hands cross the midline.

Remember that imaginary line of long axis rotation? Picture crossing it with your hand when the hand enters. Crossing the midline like this causes you to waste energy bringing your hand back to where an effective pull can start. This flaw impinges on the shoulder joint, too, and can cause injury. Some swimmers cross on both sides, some on one side only. As an added problem the hips usually go out in opposition, creating unwanted drag. This flaw is also responsible for shortening your stroke, because the lateral motion of your arm sacrifices extension in front.

Rx: single-arm drills (page 51) and catch-up drill (page 52)

SYMPTOM: insufficient arm extension

Almost all swimmers fail to extend fully in front on their arm entry. This extension is critical for maximizing your stroke length.

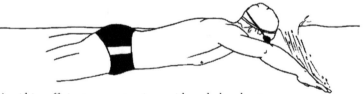

Avoid insufficient arm extension, with early hand entry.

You may remember that good arm extension in front is the result of driving your arm forward from your shoulder, and of rotation of your body along the long axis—in fact, a large part of arm extension is created by this rotation.

Rx: single-arm drills (page 51), catch-up drill (page 52), and count-stroke drill (page 47)

SYMPTOM: incomplete stroke finish

You can lose as much as half a foot to a foot (15 to 30 cm) of stroke length by not finishing your stroke fully. Too many swimmers take their hands out too early, thus missing some of the most effective part of the pull.

Avoid incomplete stroke finish, with early hand exit.

Remember, the pull (adduction) is a two-part phase—the second part being this extension, or finish. The finish uses your triceps muscle to extend your arm completely, with your hand still accelerating. Missing out on the finish will consequently rob you of speed. This common flaw is likely to pop up when you get tired.

Rx: single-arm drills (page 51), count-stroke drill (page 47), and thumb-scrape drill (page 51)

SYMPTOM: dropped elbow during pull (adduction)

Probably the largest loss of power—and hence speed—comes from not maintaining a high elbow under the water.

This loss occurs if you drop your elbow during the pull phase and end up pulling with just your hand, rather than the large paddle of your forearm and hand. Only if per-

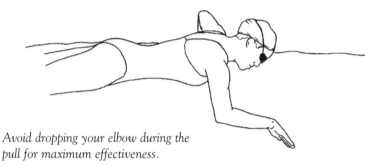

Avoid dropping your elbow during the pull for maximum effectiveness.

formed correctly—with this large paddle to pull against the water—can the pull employ your large lat muscles, and utilize your physiology. Assume you drop your elbow, though. Chances are you do, and only with underwater video can you know for sure.

Rx: fist drill (page 45), single-arm drills (page 51), and catch-up drill (page 52)

SYMPTOM: poor or no long axis rotation

Another very common flaw that robs swimmers of power is poor or no long axis rotation. Most often, the problem occurs when your rotation stops at your hips; fishtailing results. If no rotation occurs, you swim "flat." The result of flat swimming is short, ineffective strokes.

Remember that in swimming, as in many sports, power comes from your hips. Rotating your hips allows you to get

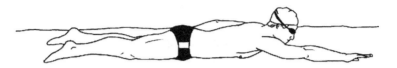

Avoid swimming flat, or without long axis rotation.

your whole body involved. Your extension and finish are also enhanced by good rotation along your long axis.

Rx: catch-up drill (page 52) and kick-on-side drill (page 49)

SYMPTOM: lack of shoulder rotation

The other common but more subtle rotational flaw is a lack or absence of shoulder rotation. Without this, your strokes are short and fast. You usually look rushed and stiff while swimming.

The elliptical rotation of your shoulder can, if done correctly, gain you another 2 to 3 inches (5 to 10 cm) of stroke length.

Rx: single-arm drills (page 51), catch-up drill (page 52), and count-stroke drill (page 47)

SYMPTOM: poor head position

Most swimmers with this problem dip down their heads when they breathe. Some swimmers maintain a low head position all the time. This flaw is easy to spot, because the swimmers looks like they are plowing their heads through the water.

Remember that when you are not breathing, the water should hit your forehead between hairline and goggles. If you drop your head below this position, you will create unwanted drag. Noticing where you are looking when you breathe will help: You should be gazing approximately 5

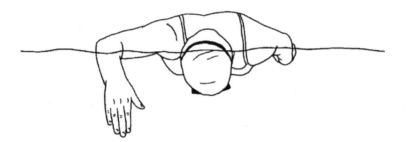

Avoid plowing your head through the water due to poor head positioning.

degrees forward of a line perpendicular to your head. A good head position allows for a good body position—as described in chapter 2.

Rx: head-up drill (page 47), and swimming (including all drills) while concentrating on feeling the water break between your goggles and the top of your forehead

S YMPTOM : incorrect hand entry

If your hand brings in air on entry it is said to be "unclean." This air needs to be pushed out of the way before you can make an effective pull, and part of your power is thus lost by pushing air bubbles. If you reach too far forward before

Avoid slapping the water on your hand entry.

slipping your hand in the water and slap it on the water, you create unnecessary turbulence and drag.

Remember to slip in your hand about 8 to 12 inches (20 to 30 cm) in front of your shoulder, and extend it under the water. Visualize a Ziploc bag lying on the surface that you want to slip your hand inside.

Rx: single-arm drills (page 51), catch-up drill (page 52), and fingertip-drag drill (page 46)

A STEP FARTHER

Once you have cured your major freestyle technique flaws and become proficient at flip turns, you may want to experiment with conscious sculling and hand angles to try to squeak out some more thrust from each stroke.

Sculling is a necessary element of all swimming strokes. As I said in the previous chapter, your long axis rotation in freestyle (and backstroke) will automatically help you to scull by causing your arm to move back and forth. Once you are rotating correctly, however, and have gained a good sense for what sculling feels like, you may want to play with your sculling a bit, to find out what works best for you.

Everyone's physiology is unique and exactly how to maximize it is learned through experiments of one—you. The best way to approach this is to have some fun. Although sculling in freestyle is often described as an S-pattern—with an outsweep, insweep, and outsweep—there is no perfect pattern. Some world class swimmers pull straight at the beginning, then insweep, then outsweep (an upside-down, question-mark pattern). Make a game out of it, and try them all.

For hand angles, use the count-stroke drill (page 47) to see what changes lower your stroke number. The min-max stroke drill (page 48) will give the most honest indication of what works. Try stroking wider or narrower, with your palm pointing slightly in or slightly out, and so on. Have fun! This type of playing with the stroke has often helped me get a breakthrough with swimmers who were at a plateau. And it can be done in all four strokes. However, never attempt any new changes close to (within 3 to 4 weeks of) a competition.

Noticing flaws on your video, then working on them, will lead you to faster, more enjoyable swimming. The flaws listed above are by no means all the errors that you might have. However, they are by far the most common ones I see at the Total Training Swim Clinics. Work on only one flaw at a time. In other words, do not work on hand entry and rotation within the same drill. Work on entry for a few drills, stop, then do some drills for rotation. Without this mental separation the drills will be much less effective. Be sure to allow some time to "not think" about the changes and let them come naturally. During main sets is the best time to let go of technique and focus on exertion level. Improving your technique is a combination of working hard on a change, then letting go. These changes take time, so be patient and persistent. After a week or two revideo yourself and see how you are progressing.

Technique training is an ongoing process, and at first it may seem like drudgery, but in fact the ongoing process is what makes swimming exciting. You can look forward to always improving, even as you age. How does the phrase "ageless athlete" sound? The majority of masters swimmers swim faster as they age. Of course there is an upper limit physically (it is older than you think). Are these older athletes stronger? Sometimes. Usually they are smarter. Allow yourself to get fascinated by this idea. Read books, read magazines, watch videos, and whenever possible watch swim meets. Better yet, enter one!

4

DRILLS, DRILLS, DRILLS

Repetition is the mother of skill.

The best way to effect changes in your freestyle technique is to perform stroke drills—the tools for improving your swimming. When doing drills it is important to concentrate on the change you want to effect. Going through the motions of the drills is not enough. Instead you must focus your attention on the desired change. Breaking a habit that has most likely been around for awhile is not done unconsciously.

Fins will be of great assistance in all of the drills (with the exception of the fist drill and the thumb-scrape drill). Because of the slower—sometimes singular—movements they involve, drills are significantly slower than regular swimming. The fins will help you maintain speed, so that you do not practice with a body position different from your usual one. The best fins are the Zoomer™ Fins. They will give you added speed, and allow you to keep your kick small. More on fins in chapter 6.

Drills must be performed at every workout. They serve to remind your nervous system of the way in which you intend to move your body. Drills should be performed after your warm-up, and before your cooldown. Chapter 7 will show you exactly how to incorporate drills into your workout. There are many different types of drills—each for a specific problem. As an example, fist swimming is the best way to work on attaining and maintaining a high elbow.

After having read chapter 3, you should have a list of drills prescribed for your own flaws. If your list is long, then just start out with one or two drills. Anywhere from two to four pool lengths is a good distance for a drill, before either changing to a different drill or repeating the same one again. Some drills can help you work on more than one flaw, but doing a drill for one flaw does not count for any others. The best two words I can say to you are: Be specific.

FIST DRILL

How?

This drill is performed by swimming a normal freestyle stroke—with the slight change of making a fist with each hand. Feel the pressure from the water on your forearm. For best results, open your hand in the middle of a lap: Do one-and-a-half lengths, then open your hand immediately. You will realize how powerful you are with a bent elbow under the water.

Why?

This drill helps you maintain a high elbow (underwater), which allows you to employ your powerful back muscles for your pull. The reason this drill works is that it *forces* you to bend your elbow and use your forearm. You can get away with a low elbow if you are using an open hand.

When? How much?

Do this during the stroke-drill section of your workout, two lengths at a time. Swim one-and-a-half lengths with fists, then open your hand. Repeat this sequence 2 to 3 times. This is also an excellent drill to do between sets due to the fact that we all tend to drop our elbow as we fatigue. In this case, just one sequence is enough.

FINGERTIP-DRAG DRILL

How?

To perform this drill, drag your fingertips across the water on the recovery. This requires you to relax your hand and maintain a high elbow. Drop your hand in when it starts to feel heavy. Stay on your side as long as possible; as your hand enters the water, rotate to the other side.

Why?

This drill helps you keep a high elbow on the recovery phase of your arm cycle; keeps your hand from recovering too high and slapping the water; helps you work on a smooth and clean (no-air) hand entry; and helps you stay on your side longer (works rotation).

When? How much?

The fingertip-drag drill should be performed within the framework of the stroke-drill section of your workout. Two lengths at a time is optimum. Do one to three sets of this drill.

HEAD-UP SWIMMING DRILL

How?

Swim freestyle with your head out of the water looking straight ahead. A variation is to swing your head from side to side as you breathe.

Why?

This drill helps you improve your body position. It is also helpful in keeping a high head position. If you plan on doing open-water swimming, this drill should be a regular part of your workout: Its technique is invaluable to navigating in choppy water. It is a strenuous drill, and it may take some time before you are able to complete an entire lap. Do a few strokes at a time, and work into it.

When? How much?

Before or after the main set is a good time to perform this drill. Since it is strenuous, do one length at a time.

COUNT-STROKE DRILL

How?

Swim one length of the pool, counting the number of strokes you take. Your goal is to take as few as possible. Try to get the most from each stroke and be as streamlined as possible. It is O.K. to glide a little, and to make your stroke as long as possible. Use long axis rotation to lengthen your stroke, and take powerful pulls.

Why?

This drill helps you lengthen your stroke and play with sculling. Some swimmers rush through their strokes— counting helps them slow down.

When? How Much?

This is a great drill to do before and after your main set. Try to keep a P.R. (personal record) so that you have a number to track.

MIN-MAX DRILL

How?

This is a variation of the count-stroke drill in which you time your swim—usually one length of it, although two lengths works as well. Add your time to the number of strokes you take. Example: A 50-yard time of 30 seconds with 28 strokes produces a min-max of 58. As you can see, there are two ways to bring your number down.

Why?

Min-max makes sure you do not overglide and swim so slow that the drill becomes a game of delaying the stroke as long as possible, and taking glides that are ineffective when swimming. Min-max really keeps you honest, and teaches you what length of stroke is the most efficient.

This drill is terrific, because it gives you real numbers to tell you how you are doing. Get excited, have fun, and learn how to continually improve your P.R.

When? How much?

Again, this is a great drill to do before and after your main set; you can even do it as a main set of 50s. Remember to keep track of your min-max P.R.

KICK-ON-SIDE DRILL

How?

This drill essentially consists of a regular flutter kick, performed on your side. Lay out on your side (in the water); put your bottom arm out in front of you, and your top arm on your side. You can start by swimming an entire lap on one side, but as you get proficient you will want to do 6 to 10 kicks on one side, then alternate. This rotation is initiated by your arm and shoulders, followed by your torso, hips, and, finally, legs. Do not let the fact that I have described this as a segmented movement allow you to do it slowly. As you get comfortable doing this drill, try to initiate the rotation from your kick. Alternating from one side to the other should be a snapping, sharp, total-body movement.

Why?

This drill will help you improve your rotation along the long axis, and help you build kicking endurance. It forces you to rotate your entire body, not just your torso, while kicking correctly. The way you kick with a kickboard is not the way you should kick while swimming, which makes using one a poor flutter-kick-training technique.

When? How much?

I suggest you do this drill in a four-length sequence as follows:

One length right side only

One length left side only

Two lengths alternating sides, six kicks on each

Do a few (1 to 5) of these four-length sequences after stroke drills and before your main set.

KICK-ON-BACK DRILL

How?

This drill consists of a backstroke kick—the flutter kick on your back. Alternate one leg coming up (upbeat) and one leg going down (downbeat). As in your freestyle kick, point your toes and move your legs by using the upper muscles of your legs, hips, and buttocks. Your hands may be either at your sides or stretched out overhead in a streamlined position.

Why?

This drill helps balance your muscle development. In all forms of physical training, it is helpful to work muscles in opposing motions.

When? How much?

This is a good drill (along with the kick-on-side drill) to do after warm-up. You can do sets in 50s, 100s, or 200s. This drill is also helpful used as a break from the main set. It can offer a refreshing change that gives some over-worked muscles a chance to rejuvenate. As with almost all of the other drills, fins will help you get the most out of it.

THUMB-SCRAPE DRILL

How?

As the name implies, in this drill you scrape your thigh with your thumb as you finish your pull and start your recovery.

Why?

Because you have to fully extend and use your triceps muscle to brush your thigh, this drill guarantees that you finish your strokes.

When? How much?

Perform this drill anytime you feel your strokes may be short and ineffective. One to two lengths of the pool is usually sufficient to remind you to finish fully.

SINGLE-ARM DRILL

How?

In this drill you swim with one arm only—either left or right. The arm not being used stays extended in front, while the other strokes. You should always use fins in this drill, because the action of using one arm will make you move significantly more slowly in the water than when you swim normally.

Why?

This drill is terrific because it allows you to concentrate on one arm at a time. You can actually watch your arm as you take it through the five phases of the arm cycle.

When? How much?

Two to three 100s of each single-arm stroke (left and right) is best done after your warm-up and before your cooldown as part of your basic stroke drill.

CATCH-UP DRILL

How?

When performing this drill you wait for one hand to enter before pulling with the other. It is like performing alternating single-arm drills.

Why?

This is an excellent drill in helping you improve your rotation. It also helps you work on your rhythm. "Swimming rhythm" is another way of saying the timing of your pull, kick, and glide. This is different for every individual, and is perfected by experimentation. This drill is the most helpful for allowing you to experiment and to feel relaxed and comfortable in the water.

When? How much?

As with the single-arm drill, this drill should be performed as part of your basic stroke drill, after your warm up and before your cooldown. Two to three 100s is a good amount.

■ ■ ■

With these three drills—the left and right single-arm drills, and the catch-up drill—you can perform a basic

---

DRILL SUMMARY

DRILL NAME	IMPROVES	PAGE
Fist drill	elbow flexion	45
Fingertip-drag drill	entry/recovery/rotation	46
Head-up swimming drill	head/body position	47
Count-stroke drill	stroke length	47
Min-max drill	stroke efficiency	48
Kick-on-side drill	rotation/kick	49
Kick-on-back drill	balance/kick/rotation	50
Thumb-scrape drill	stroke finish	51
Single-arm drill	all phases of arm cycle	51
Catch-up drill	rotation/extension	52

---

stroke drill that should become a standard part of your workout. The reason I refer to this as the "basic" stroke drill is that it allows you to work on a myriad of stroke corrections: hand entry, rotation, head position, elbow flexion, and so on. Do not neglect the special drills, however, as they are tailor-designed to work on specific corrections.

The basic stroke drill should be done in the following sequence:

One lap right arm only

One lap left arm only

One lap catch-up stroke

One lap whole stroke

The object of the basic stroke drill is to first work on each side individually and specifically; next work on rotation; and finally put it all together with whole-stroke or regular swimming.

DESIGNING THE DRILL PORTION OF YOUR WORKOUT

As you can probably see, the stroke and kick drills are best performed after your warm-up and before your cooldown. Ideally, perform two to three 100s of the basic stroke drill, and one to two 100s of specific stroke drills (like fist or thumb-scrape). Before each sequence, ask yourself what specific aspect of your stroke you would like to focus on. After these stroke drills, do a couple 100s of kicking drills.

You will swim significantly more slowly when performing drills, because you are breaking up the stroke and concentrating on form. This is why, as I have said before, it is helpful to use fins to help maintain your speed. The problem with going more slowly is that it changes the dynamics (your body position, and all the angles of your pull) of your stroke. You do not want to spend time and effort perfecting a stroke that in the end is different than the one you will be swimming with. You can use a pull buoy when you want to really focus in on upper-body technique and not be distracted by kicking. Try to keep up your speed on drills, although their emphasis is technique. But also be careful not to let what I just said make you rush your stroke. You need to take your time working on stroke correction. Again, this is why fins are helpful. Devices like fins and pull buoys are discussed thoroughly in chapter 6.

If this is the first time you have heard of drills you may feel inundated. Do not be overwhelmed—just dive in and take it stroke by stroke. Performing some of these drills may feel like learning a new stroke; be patient, and you will get it in a short amount of time.

Remember, drills are the tools for improving and maintaining good freestyle technique. The best swimmers in the world perform drills, so if you do, too, you will be in good company. This is the cerebral part of swimming. You are training your motor neuron pathways and you must visualize the changes before you make them. It is usually helpful to go through the motions on a bench before doing them in the water. As with any other motor skill change, time and repetition are required. The longer you have been swimming incorrectly, the more repetition you will need to make the new way natural. You know the saying: "Repetition is the mother of skill."

You may at first feel like swimming drills are awkward, maybe even "weird." That is a good sign: It means you are doing something different. To see if different is better, get videotaped again and compare your new stroke to your old. Armed with drills you can see where your technique is flawed, apply the drills, and enjoy improved swimming.

5

BREASTSTROKE, BACKSTROKE, AND BUTTERFLY

There are four main swimming strokes: freestyle, breaststroke, backstroke, and butterfly. Due to the popularity and versatility of freestyle, I have spent a larger portion of time on it. Freestyle is the fastest and one of the easier strokes to learn (breaststroke is the easiest), and that is what causes its popularity.

This chapter is devoted to the three other strokes—often referred to as the "off-strokes." There is good reason to master these, even if you think you are not interested in them for fitness or competition. Namely, they use different muscle groups and help balance your muscular development. Another benefit of these off-strokes is that they can help you develop that elusive "feel for the water"—the feeling that you are moving still water, as opposed to water already moving. These strokes will be discussed in the same format as freestyle, with sections on arm cycle and stroke, rotation, body position, kicking, breathing, and turns. I will then point out some technique areas to focus on.

Many of the principles that apply to freestyle apply to the off-strokes. Streamlining to reduce drag is a constant principle in all four strokes. Bending the elbow at a 90-degree angle during your pull phase is another. A third is accelerating through the pull. In all strokes you start "soft" and finish "hard."

BREASTSTROKE

Breaststroke is the oldest swimming stroke. I wonder if that means we were all frogs years ago? It is often considered a more relaxing stroke than the other three, and has two noncompetitive cousins—sidestroke and elementary backstroke. Sidestroke is a form of breaststroke performed on your side; elementary backstroke is a breaststroke performed on your back (a connection similar to that between freestyle and backstroke). Many new swimmers find learning breaststroke easier than freestyle. If you feel very awkward with freestyle then try breaststroke as a stepping-stone.

This stroke was (and still is) very well suited for rivers, lakes, and oceans where the swimmer could expect rough water. It allows you to use less effort, and enables you to keep your head out of the water. The reduced effort comes from the stroke's long glide, and its use of the large, powerful leg muscles. The head-up position allows for comfortable, normal breathing and the ability to see where you are going. It is a good stroke to know when swimming in open-water competitions because it allows you to sight your course and continue swimming at the same time.

Due to innovative swimmers constantly improving swimming, the breaststroke has had to be saved from extinction as a competitive event at least three times. First, around the turn of the century, the invention of the crawl (freestyle) temporarily caused breaststroke to disappear from competition. Eventually, however, breaststroke was defined as its own stroke. Next, in the 1930s, breaststroke was temporarily sidelined by the invention of a new stroke called "butterfly." Eventually rule changes made butterfly the fourth and final competitive stroke. Then, the Japanese discovered that they could swim breaststroke faster under-water; that changed the whole event. Eventually, around 1957, the rules were changed to outlaw more than one stroke and pull (per lap) underwater.

As you can see, the rules for breaststroke are constantly changing as swimmers invent new movements. Competitive swimming's governing board must decide whether each change will become part of "legal" breaststroke, or become a movement that could disqualify a swimmer. But despite all this, the ancient art of breaststroke has stood the test of time.

The slowest of the four strokes, breaststroke relies heavily on the kick, and therefore develops the legs more than any other stroke.

ARM CYCLE

There are four phases to the breaststroke arm cycle: recovery, elbow flexion, pull, and inward sweep. To begin

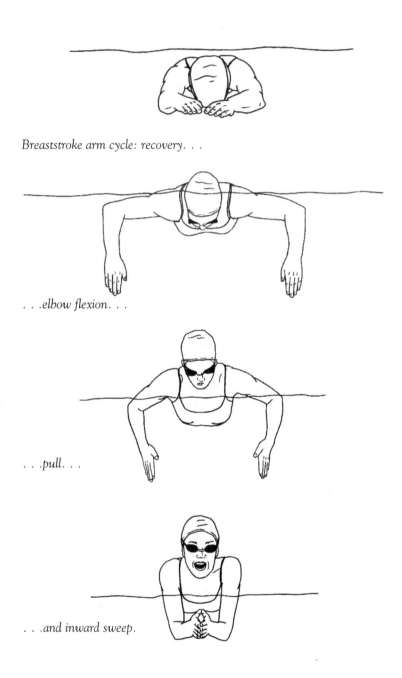

Breaststroke arm cycle: recovery. . .

. . .elbow flexion. . .

. . .pull. . .

. . .and inward sweep.

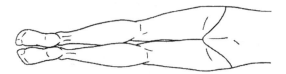

Breaststroke kick: legs together. . .

. . .drawing knees up to chest. . .

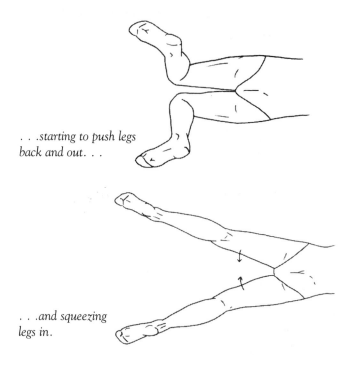

. . .starting to push legs back and out. . .

. . .and squeezing legs in.

the recovery, place your hands in a praying position, palms facing each other, just under your chin. As you drive your arms forward, keep your hands together. As your arms start to reach full extension, turn your palms down.

Elbow flexion, as in freestyle, is very important. After turning your palms down, bend your arms at the elbows and sweep them out to the outside of your shoulders. Your hands should be constantly adjusting so as to be perpendicular to the direction of limb movement. This sounds much more complicated than it is. As you sweep out, your hand angle pitches to make the resultant force backward, hence propel you forward.

The pull provides the bulk of your forward propulsion. This pull is the same as the pull (adduction) in freestyle. The only difference is that you do not finish it (except on the one underwater pull at the beginning of each lap). Stop just past the shoulders, with your elbows still bent.

During the inward sweep you finally sweep your arms in, bringing your palms together. You now are ready for your next stroke.

In your breaststroke arm cycle, avoid the temptation to pull back too far. This extra pull is not worth the increased drag of breaststroke's underwater recovery.

Ever since the invention of butterfly, the rules for breaststroke have stated that your arms must stay underwater or on the surface. It comes as no surprise that recent breaststroke rule changes allow partial recovery above the water, but if the elbows break the water you get disqualified. Most breaststrokers now perform a wave breaststroke that uses an undulating motion. Yes, you guessed it, times are faster.

Rotation

There is no long axis rotation in breaststroke, but there is that forward elliptical rotation of the shoulders. As in freestyle, this helps you get your arms out farther, for longer pulls.

Body position

As in freestyle, the ideal breaststroke body position is fairly flat with a slight upward angle. You will have some up-and-down motion in this stroke—it is necessary for breathing.

Kicking

The breaststroke kick can be described as the "frog kick." It is performed by drawing your knees up toward your chest, then pushing your legs out, back, and in. There are two main movements—the recovery, in which you bend your knees (and hips, slightly) and bring your legs up toward your body, and the actual thrust, in which you straighten your legs with an accelerating movement. Your feet start in a flexed position, and end in a pointed position when the legs come together. It is important to squeeze your legs together completely, and to point your toes at the end of the kick. This kick differs from all other swim kicks in that it takes place in the horizontal plane, moving laterally. All the other kicks are in the vertical plane, moving up and down.

Breathing

The breath in breaststroke occurs in the middle of phase four of the arm cycle, while your arms are sweeping in.

Your legs should be drawing up, getting into position to kick back.

PUSH-OFFS AND TURNS

The breaststroke push-off is the same as the freestyle in terms of streamlining off the wall. After that you take a pull, then a kick, underwater. Come up to breathe as you start your second stroke.

Unlike freestyle, only an open turn is allowed in breaststroke, and you need to touch the wall with both hands. Simply drop one hand after touching and pivot around for a push-off.

TIPS FOR BREASTSTROKE

To put your breaststroke together you need to time your pull, kick, breath, and glide. Start by getting a good, streamlined push-off. Then take a pull, followed by a kick, followed by a glide. Start the kick as your hands come together. As you finish the kick, you are pushing your hands through to the front.

The timing of your glide length is crucial. Take enough time to feel your speed, then begin your next pull as you start to slow down. Experiment with your glide length and with the timing of your breath, pull, and kick. Be patient; getting this right takes time. I suggest watching swimmers perform or, better yet, getting a swimming video and watching in slow motion.

BACKSTROKE

The backstroke was a leisure stroke until the beginning of this century. It was never used in competition because it was slow. When it was made an official stroke, the only rule was to stay on your back. The stroke has since evolved to resemble freestyle—but on your back. It is interesting to note that with today's better technique and training, backstroke is now more or less the same speed as butterfly, making it second in speed to freestyle.

Backstroke is distinguished from the other three strokes by the fact that it is, of course, performed on your back. Getting your face out of the water and taking in the sights is a nice feeling (outside, sunny pools require tinted goggles). Backstroke is a little more natural to learn than the other strokes because we instinctively want to float on our backs. After we learn to float on our backs we paddle around in different ways or simply kick.

Backstroke is a great break from freestyle, and helps balance your freestyle muscles. Despite the commonalities—like rotation, and the fact that the backstroke kick is just the freestyle flutter kick performed on your back—thinking of backstroke as "freestyle on your back" is a little too simplistic.

Arm cycle

There are four phases to the backstroke arm cycle: entry, elbow flexion, pull, and recovery. The phases are very similar to those of freestyle, except that the release phase is absent since the finish of backstroke puts your hand in the proper position for recovery.

The entry point for backstroke is almost directly in front of your shoulder. Your hand enters pinkie first, with the elbow straight. As your hand enters it reaches forward through the long axis and shoulder rotations (as in

Backstroke arm cycle: entry. . .

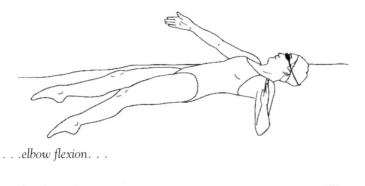

. . .elbow flexion. . .

. . .pull (arm extension). . .

. . .and recovery.

freestyle); your palm rotates so that it faces the bottom of the pool.

As in freestyle, elbow flexion is extremely important: It provides that large paddle surface (hand and forearm) for maximum power. Long axis rotation is key to allowing for the bend in your elbow. Try to keep extending your shoulder forward as you bend your elbow. This will make your stroke as long as possible.

Elbow flexion is followed by the pull or adduction, in which you pull your arm along your body. As your hand passes your shoulder, start to extend your arm; use your triceps to finish the stroke, pushing your hand down. As in freestyle, there is a sculling motion that is aided by your long axis rotation. You are now ready for the recovery.

The recovery phase is similar to that of freestyle. It is the rest phase, during which your hand moves from the end of the stroke to the beginning of another. It differs from that of freestyle in that you keep a straight elbow.

ROTATION

Rotation in backstroke is the same as in freestyle—both long axis rotation and shoulder rotation occur simultaneously. Both are instrumental in ensuring a correct pull, causing sculling, and generating power. Along your long axis, as in freestyle, your hips and legs need to rotate with your upper body; the backstroke shoulder rotation movement is the same as in freestyle except in the opposite direction—a backward shrug as opposed to a forward one.

BODY POSITION

The body position in backstroke is again horizontal with a slight upward angle, the head at the higher point. Be as stretched out as possible. A common error in backstroke is bending at the waist—almost sitting in the water. This position creates drag and does not float you as well as a straighter one. Tucking your chin can lead to this flaw. The ideal backstroke body position is to have the waterline break at the crown of your head.

KICKING

The backstroke kick is an upside down flutter kick (the kick used in freestyle). The kick should be small and remain in the slipstream, for the same reasons the freestyle kick should.

BREATHING

Nothing need be said here except that you should breathe normally, since your head is out of the water at all times.

PUSH-OFFS AND TURNS

The backstroke push-off is like the freestyle in that you want to streamline as much as possible, and stretch your arms forward locked on top of each other. Allow yourself to drop under the water and plant your feet firmly before pushing off. Use your kick to take you up to the surface.

Turning in backstroke is tricky because you have your back to the wall. Counting your strokes is one way to know where you are. If the pool you are in has lane lines, they too can help you determine where the end of the pool is.

Most lane lines are of alternating colors until a few yards from the end of the pool, where they turn to a solid color. You can see this in your peripheral vision as you swim backstroke. Ever wonder why "grand opening flags" are draped across a pool, five yards from each end? It is another way to let backstrokers know that they are 3 to 5 strokes from the wall.

Competition rules have recently been changed to allow you to take one stroke on your stomach before flipping. This has made for faster times. Basically, rotate onto your stomach and perform a freestyle flip turn (see chapter 2). Then come off on your back.

BUTTERFLY

Butterfly is the newest racing stroke and thus has a short history. It has only been a separate stroke since 1952—just 20 years before Mr. Fly himself, Mark Spitz, crushed his competitors at the Munich Olympics. Butterfly has its origins in breaststroke. In 1933, a breaststroker tried making a recovery over the surface of the water and found it faster. Soon all breaststrokers were doing this, while retaining the breaststroke kick. Later, when the dolphin kick was developed, butterfly became a separate stroke and the rules for breaststroke were changed to make sure the arms stayed in the water. Although butterfly is an offshoot of breaststroke, its arm action and kick are very much like those of freestyle.

Arguably it is the most beautiful of the four strokes. The beauty of butterfly has been compared to that of a dolphin undulating in the water. Beauty comes at a price, however—butterfly is hard to learn and do. A fast and powerful stroke, it is usually performed in shorter sets than the other strokes due to its increased strenuousness. For short distances, it is second in speed to freestyle. Most fitness swimmers skip this stroke—and so miss a potentially rewarding experience. Butterfly is so enjoyable to watch and do when performed correctly that it is almost an art form. Besides the stroke's beauty, it allows you to really work your muscles, building them stronger than you can with the other strokes. Butterflyers are usually noticeably more muscular than other swimmers. Lap for lap, butterfly ("fly" for short) will give you the workout of your life. Give it a try if you never have; if you already know it, but have been avoiding it, go for it.

ARM CYCLE

Although the phases of the butterfly arm cycle seem confusing, they are very similar to those of the freestyle; the exception is that your arms trace a pattern no longer facilitated by long axis rotation. The four phases of the arm cycle in fly are: entry, elbow flexion, pull, and recovery.

Your hands should enter 8 to 12 inches (20 to 30 cm) in front of, and just outside, your shoulders. The fly entry is just like the freestyle, with the twist that you use both arms together. Since you have no long axis rotation in fly, you need to use shoulder rotation and undulating motion to extend your arms far forward.

The butterfly elbow flexion movement is almost identical to the freestyle. Try to keep your elbow as high as possible to prepare for the pull to come.

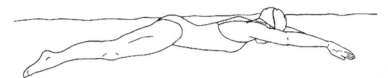

Butterfly: Starting from a streamlined position, begin undulating the hips down and pulling your hands out to the side.

As your arms begin elbow flexion, the kick is coming up slightly.

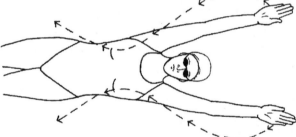

The pull pattern creates the outline of an hourglass.

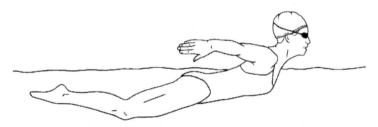

The recovery occurs as the legs kick down, helping to raise the upper part of the body.

The pull is, once again, similar to freestyle's, but you want to consciously move your arms in an S-pattern as you pull back. Some coaches describe this as an "hourglass" shape since both arms move simultaneously, but there is no perfect model for it. The idea is to go out, in, and out so that you take advantage of the sculling effect to find still water, and generate more lift and forward propulsion. At the end of the pull, extend fully (as in freestyle); finish by straightening out your elbows. At the very end, turn out your hand slightly to release your shoulder (this is described as a separate phase in freestyle). This release prepares you for an injury-free recovery.

The recovery is a double-action freestyle recovery. Lead with your elbow until your hand and elbow reach your shoulder area. Then your hand leads the way back to another entry. The timing of your breathing is key to a relaxed recovery. If your timing is wrong, your recovery will be very strenuous.

ROTATION

Because butterfly utilizes both sides of the body at once, it involves no long axis body rotation. It thus relies heavily on shoulder rotation—the same forward shrug movement as in freestyle. Fly's shoulder rotation can be perfectly simulated by doing forward shoulder shrugs with light dumbbells.

KICKING

Fly uses what is known as a "dolphin kick"—both legs kick together in an undulating motion. As with breaststroke, the timing of the pull and kick is critical. There are two kicks to every pull in butterfly. Imagine you are pushing off the wall and are in the streamlined position. As you reach the surface, kick down. As you start the pull, kick up. The kick down helps you get your body out of the water and take a breath (facing forward) while performing the recovery of the stroke. As your hand enters the water, your head follows—creating butterfly's characteristic undulating movement. Practicing the kick alone with a kickboard can often help you get the feeling of undulation. As with breaststroke, the best way to study fly is to watch others and/or slow-motion video. To understand the undulating motion, watching dolphins can be inspiring. There are world class butterfly swimmers who have swum with dolphins to gain knowledge.

BREATHING

The breathing in butterfly is integrated with the entire stroke, and timing is critical. Use the downbeat of your kick to help you lift up your body to breathe. Drop your head for the recovery, to allow your arms to reach out in front. Some swimmers, such as Melvin Stewart, breathe to the side in fly and thus have less need to go up and down. Try it both ways—head in front and then, in a way that resembles freestyle breathing, to the side.

PUSH-OFFS AND TURNS

The push-off in butterfly is the same as in freestyle, except you need to undulate and pump the dolphin kick. Time your first stroke to have a powerful downbeat kick to get you up for the breath. The turn is like a breaststroke turn, requiring a two-handed touch. After the touch, drop one hand and perform a push-off.

THE MEDLEY

The competitive event known as the "medley" is raced over a distance of 200 or 400 meters or yards and consists of an equal number of laps of the four strokes I have described, in this order: butterfly, backstroke, breaststroke, and freestyle. Whether your goal is to race a medley or to swim for fun and fitness, the three off-strokes are important and have the cross-training effect of helping with the other strokes. A few laps of backstroke and breaststroke between sets or after your warm-up can really make you feel great. If change is the spice of life, then off-strokes are the spice of swimming. Use the spices of backstroke, breaststroke, and butterfly to add variety to your swimming. Who knows? You may end up finding these strokes more enjoyable than freestyle.

6

SWIMMING
AIDS

The right tool for the right job.

Did you ever see the person who shows up at the pool with a scuba catch bag containing fins, paddles, buoy, and kickboard? Ever wonder if any of that stuff is useful? This chapter will help you sort out which of these swimming aids are helpful, which are harmful, and which other products you can put to good use.

SWIMSUIT

Not absolutely necessary, but a good idea for public pools. Use snug-fitting, nylon or lycra suits to reduce drag and allow good feel of the water. Avoid wearing loose articles (like gym shorts, etc.).

SWIM CAP

Swim caps, tight latex caps worn on swimmers' heads, are important for several reasons: They help protect the hair

from chlorine and sun; they provide some heat retention (important in cold water) and some drag reduction; and, most importantly, they allow swimmers to feel the water around their heads and shoulders. This helps you keep your head in a good position, and is of paramount importance if you have long hair. With long hair swirling around your head and neck, it is virtually impossible to feel the waterline on your head. Most swimming pools require a cap if your hair is past your ears, for sanitary reasons.

GOGGLES

The invention of goggles made swimming much more enjoyable for leisure swimmers—no more chlorine irritation. For competitors, goggles led the way to the mega-yardage of the '70s and '80s—they were responsible for huge drops in swimming records. Goggles come in different shapes, sizes, and lens tints. Tint is a matter of personal preference; the darker or mirrored tints are better for outdoor swimming. Fit is the key for goggles. Finding a good fit is not always easy, since all our eye sockets are a little different. If your goggles do not fit well, they will leak. When they fit correctly you will feel a slight suction. My best advice is to try as many different styles as possible. When you find a style that fits well, stock up.

PADDLES

Swim paddles, which come in different shapes and sizes, are plastic
paddles slightly larger than your
hand and fastened to it with surgical
tubing. Their purpose is to increase
the surface area of your pull, thereby
increasing the resistance against which
you stroke. Paddles can be helpful in drill work because
they amplify any slight change in your hand angle as you
pull. A coach may prescribe that you perform part of a set
with paddles alone, or with paddles and a pull buoy,
because he or she wants you to overload your muscles.

Use paddles with caution. The most common swimming injury is swimmer's shoulder—technically, tendonitis
of the shoulder, an inflammation of the tendons surround-
ing the shoulder. Swimming is very repetitive and if your
arm comes too far over with each stroke, and/or you do not
release well after each stroke, your tendon (connection
between muscle and bone) can rub on bony prominences
and/or other areas, thereby causing inflammation. This is
one of the many reasons why proper technique is so important. Using paddles to practice any but the best strokes is
asking for an overuse injury. In addition, the increased
resistance that paddles provide is effective only if your
stroke is perfect. As a rule, then, do not use paddles unless
under the supervision of a coach. Another concern with
paddles is that they can be dangerous in a crowded pool. If
you hit another swimmer while you are wearing paddles
you could cause injury.

FINS

Fins are a fun and essential aid to your swim training. They should be used during most drills: they help you keep up your speed so that you are simulating the body position you use when actually swimming. Fins also allow you to swim at a 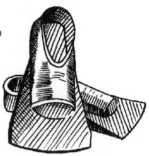 faster pace than you are capable of—indispensable when you are trying to break out of a rut and get a "feel" for swimming faster. And fins strengthen your legs and increase your ankle flexibility—both crucial to improving your kick.

There are many types of fins on the market, but the most effective is the Zoomers™ Fins. These are very short, which is what makes them so effective. They look like regular fins except that they have only a 2- to 3-inch (5 to 7 ½ cm) blade. Such short fins do not allow you to kick too big, and thus most benefit your swimming.

Reminder from chapter 2: The key to a great kick is to keep it small and fast. This is especially important when using fins.

Resist the temptation to use large scuba fins—they make you kick large kicks and thereby teach you to allow your kick to come too far out of the slipstream. In addition, pushing off the wall with regular fins can have a suction effect, holding your feet on the wall as you push off. Fins should never be used for breaststroke, because they put tremendous strain on the knee.

KICKBOARDS

Kickboards are fun to use. They allow you to be a little social and "chat" with your swimming buddies. Kickboarding is the one swimming activity that keeps your head out of the water long enough to say, "What do you feel like eating after practice?" (This is an important question. Swimming really burns those calories.) However, while kickboards are all 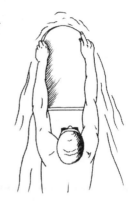 right for some of your kick training, the majority should be done by performing the kick-on-side drill (page 49). This drill allows you to work on your body rotation at the same time as your kick—you should never kick flat the way you do when using a kickboard. For this reason, avoid doing mega-yards (swim slang for many laps) with a kickboard. Use it instead for short sprints to develop leg power and speed—or, as I mentioned, for its social aspects. And remember to kick small and fast to stay in the slipstream.

PULL BUOY

The pull buoy, a flotation device designed to fit between and float your legs, is very safe and effective for specific training and stroke work. In swimming, kicking not only provides forward propulsion

but also keeps your legs up, thereby reducing drag. When performing a stroke drill and concentrating on lengthening out your stroke, it is easy to get distracted by the amount of energy you are expending to maintain your speed by kicking. Pull buoys allow you to really work on your stroke deficiencies without worrying about swimming fast enough to keep your legs afloat. Using pull buoys during drills—like using fins—helps you maintain a better body position. Fins are a slightly better choice for drills, because they increase your speed and work your leg muscles. But sometimes— when your legs are tired from running or weightlifting, for example—using the buoy to train without having to use your legs is a nice option. Runners and people who have low body fat usually find the buoy a saving grace in getting their body positions right. If this is you, just make sure you do not become too dependent on the pull buoy. I have worked with several swimmers who always swim with a pull buoy and thus have never learned to kick properly. Though dependency is not the worst flaw you can have, swimming in its entirety—including the kick—provides a much better, more complete workout.

WET SUIT

The main purpose of the wet suit—a snug-fitting, full-body suit (sometimes with short legs and short sleeve arms—a "shorty")—is to provide warmth, but as a side benefit it increases your buoyancy. It is called a "wet suit" because a thin layer of water enters between the suit and your skin. This water quickly warms to your body temperature and keeps you warm. Wet suits are made of neoprene, a rubbery material that floats very well. The legs get the most lift from the neoprene. You can practice swimming with a wet suit by swimming with a buoy, which simulates the added buoyancy of the wet suit and allows you to not kick; this gets you accustomed to this body position without putting wear and tear on your wet suit. There are many good swimming wet suits on the market. Make sure you purchase one that was designed for swimming: Diving and surfing wet suits usually do not allow you enough freedom to move your arms and rotate properly. If you live in the North, a wet suit will extend your open-water swimming season. Be careful with your wet suit—always rinse it with fresh water, and do not store it in a hot, dry area. If you are swimming in warm water (above 75 degrees F—24 degrees C), a wet suit can cause you to dehydrate. In situations such as this, drink plenty of water before and after your swim.

TETHERS

The tether, a line (very strong rubber tube) attached to a belt and then to a ladder or some other stationary object on the pool deck, is another helpful swimming aid. There are many ways to use the swimming tether. One terrific application is to use it to turn a pool that is too small for laps into a "swimmer's treadmill." Although this may be a little boring, with the advent of waterproof radios you could get

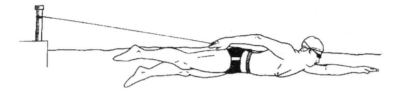

into a groove and have yourself a nice workout in a pool that would otherwise be useless. Tethers are also a great way to do extra-resistance training. The tether's springlike property allows you to set it up so that it is difficult—but not impossible—for you to reach the other end of the pool. Performing a series of these one-length "power" sprints will build tremendous strength. When you reach the far side you can swim back with the power of the tether pulling you forward—another opportunity to swim faster than you ordinarily can (your first was with fins). This gives you a taste of how your body will move when you really can swim that fast. What is great about the tether is that you start off fast, then the resistance increases slowly. Coach Dave Ferris of the Long Island Aquatic Club has produced some very fast sprinters in part because, for a period of six to eight weeks, he has them perform tethered swimming three times a week. You can do it on your own, but since it is so strenuous a coach's motivation helps you give it 100 percent.

COUNTERCURRENT POOLS

One swimming aid that will not fit into your bag and is beyond many swimmers' budgets is the swimmer's treadmill. A "personal pool" is so convenient and helpful that if you cannot afford it now, you should save up for it. Your own personal lap pool—what a concept! Not a big

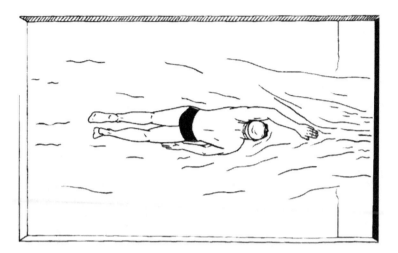

one—this is a small tank that has a current running against you. The idea here is to provide an experience much like being in a small pool with a tether. A few companies make pools (as small as 8′ × 10′) that have a variable speed current generator that allows you to "swim in place." One in particular that I have used and found exceptional is made by Endless Pools, a company in Pennsylvania. This pool comes complete with filter and heater. The countercurrent is very even.

Convenience is the primary advantage to a pool such as this. However, it also allows you to work on technique by watching yourself in a mirror on the bottom—something that can otherwise only be done in a flume. Certainly you will not want to forgo the feeling of swimming laps and doing flip turns; swimming in an endless pool should therefore be combined with swimming in a conventional pool. But on a day when you have only 30 minutes to spare, and the conventional pool is 30 or so minutes away, guess who would ordinarily miss their swim? Personal pools can be assembled in a day or two and can go in a basement, on a porch, or in the ground. Some can even be used for water running and aerobics. If you can afford the $10,000-plus ticket, there is no reason not to have one.

PACE CLOCK

The best way to time your swim-ming is with a pace clock—a large clock (placed on a pool deck or mounted on a wall) that has a minute hand and a sweeping second hand. Pace clocks provide an easy way to time your interval training (see chapter 7). Swimming with a watch is O.K., but not as effective as  using the pace clock: constantly hitting buttons and looking down at your watch is distracting. And your stroke technique will suffer if you must always reach across your body to fiddle around.

Pace clocks also come in handy for monitoring your heart rate. There are heart rate monitors that work in the pool, but because their chest straps tend to slip down when I swim, I prefer to take my pulse manually. To do this, put your index finger on your carotid artery. Use the pace clock to count your pulse for six seconds, then multiply by 10. (More on heart rate in chapter 7.)

OTHER AIDS

In my experience most other aids are nothing more than gadgets—things like finger watches, watches in goggles, webbed gloves, and lap counters. If keeping track of laps is a problem for you, try counting in groups of four lengths. Or simply know your average pace and extrapolate the number of laps you have completed by the number of elapsed minutes.

Some aids, such as drag suits, can be used to add drag to your swimming. Be careful, though, with anything that forces you to swim slowly or bogs you down: It will give you a poor body position.

■　■　■

Use the swimming aids described in this chapter to spice up your swimming. Experiment with fins and pull buoys—you will find it perks up your training. The body adapts to changing stresses by getting stronger.

Now that you have solid technique and your bag of tricks, let us take a look at how to design a fun and effective swimming program.

7

SETTING UP
YOUR TRAINING PROGRAM

No discipline seems pleasant at the time, but painful. Later on, however, it produces a harvest of righteousness and peace for those who have been trained by it.

Hebrews 12:11

I f training is not producing the results you want and is not enjoyable, you will not do it. This fact holds true for all disciplined human endeavors. Sure, you can use the brute force method, but it does not provide much staying power or enthusiasm. While it is true that your workouts will never be 100 percent ear-to-ear grinning pleasure, they need to have enough exciting elements to entice you to come back for more. A successful program requires these three elements:

- Quantifiable results (specific goals)

- A plan for achieving your goals

- The discipline to carry out your plan

I will spend the least amount of time discussing discipline, since the opening quote of this chapter says it all rather eloquently, and the fact that you have read this far in the book shows you are a follow-through person.

QUANTIFIABLE RESULTS (THE "G" WORD—GOALS)

Have you heard the statistic, "95 percent of those who write down goals achieve them and only about 3 percent of the population write them down"? I invite you to join the 3 percent. Having a solid plan gives you a great advantage. Think of it as a way of stacking the odds.

Design a single-page sheet detailing the results you would like to achieve from investment (of time, energy, money, and creativity) in your swimming program. You can fill in the sheet I have provided below, or customize it as you see fit.

This example demonstrates how easy it is to get your quantifiable goals onto paper. Then you can put this paper in a prominent place where you will see it often. Even if you are skeptical, take the 5 or 10 minutes you will need to do this. I promise it will do more for you than you can imagine.

DESIRED RESULTS FROM
MY TRAINING PROGRAM

FEELING GOALS:

Physically

Emotionally

Spiritually

SPECIFIC FITNESS GOALS

GOAL	BY WHEN	WHY
1.		
2.		
3.		
4.		
5.		
6.		

What do I need to do to achieve my goals?

How will I feel when I do achieve them?

A sample completed sheet:

DESIRED RESULTS FROM
MY TRAINING PROGRAM

FEELING GOALS:

Physically *HAVE MORE ENERGY, BE STRONGER AND LEANER*

Emotionally *BE CALM AND CENTERED, ABLE TO HANDLE ANYTHING THAT COMES UP*

Spiritually *CONNECT WITH WHO I AM AND WHAT MY PURPOSE IN LIFE IS*

SPECIFIC FITNESS GOALS

GOAL	BY WHEN	WHY
1. SWIM 100 YARDS IN UNDER 1:10	2/1/96	THIS TIME SIGNIFIES BEING IN AWESOME SHAPE
2. COMPLETE THE LOCAL Y 200 LAP CHALLENGE	4/15/96	IT IS SOMETHING I HAVE NEVER DONE
3. COMPETE IN A MEET	5/1/96	THE THRILL OF COMPETITION
4. COMPLETE A TRIATHLON	7/1/97	TRIATHLON IS THE EPITOME OF FITNESS

What do I need to do to achieve my goals?

JOIN MASTERS GROUP

VIDEOTAPE MYSELF

EAT BETTER

SCHEDULE MY WEEKS ON SUNDAY EVENING TO MAKE TIME FOR WORKOUTS

How will I feel when I do achieve them?

UNSTOPPABLE

There was this man who wanted a Cadillac. He put a picture of one on his bathroom mirror. His wife made fun of him and took it down every day. Every day he put it back. One day he got the Cadillac. The next day his wife put a picture of a mink coat on the mirror.

This same type of "success form" can be used in other areas of your life—like finances. If you approach this process right you will feel as though you have already achieved your goals. Any "failures" are simply lessons. They help you adjust your plan.

PLAN FOR ACHIEVING YOUR GOALS

With your desired results in hand you can now devise a plan for your workouts. If you have the luxury of a coach and structured practices, this section will be for your reference only. If, however, you do not, and you are going it alone, this section will serve as a step-by-step guide to coaching yourself.

Technique is by far the most important area of swimming in terms of looking for improvement. All the workouts in the world will not make a short pull longer. Only stroke analysis and correction will. If you have arrived at this section without thoroughly addressing technique, I suggest you spend more time on chapters 2, 3, 4, and 5. The best workouts in the world will give marginal results with limited technique.

Technique corrections provide exponential improvement—training and workouts, on the other hand, give linear results. The content and structure of your workouts, however, must be addressed. Coupled with sound technique, great workouts make a great swimmer.

To improve in swimming you should swim three times a week over a period of 12 weeks. The bare minimum number of workouts to improve is two a week. Those who swim once a week and say, "I feel like I am always starting over," are! A large part of swimming is training your motor neurons, and that can only be done with repetition. In a well-designed program the workouts are synergistic: Each builds on the one before. For the competitive athlete, five workouts a week is optimal. Each can be completed in 30 to 60 minutes.

As a personal trainer, the greatest flaw I see in the workouts of self-coached swimmers is the absence of interval training. Long, slow swimming will make you good at long, slow swimming. Swimming hard for a long time over and over is not much better, because it does not allow you to attain a faster-than-racing pace. To top it all off, both scenarios usually result in boredom, staleness, and slower swimming. The only way the body improves is by adapting to stress—in this case I am referring to the "good" stress of overloading from an interval set. Last but not least, intervals are fun.

INTERVAL TRAINING: THE KEY TO SUCCESS

The human machine is truly remarkable in that it responds to stress by getting stronger. In using the word *stress* here I am not referring to its usual definition: a mental or emotional state that is generally bad and/or draining. Instead,

I'm referring to the good, controlled stress of smart interval training. In the words of the great philosopher Nietzsche: "That which does not kill me makes me stronger."

Every athlete knows the validity of this quote—without "feeling it" on occasion, you accomplish little. However, you also need to understand that stress without rest will "kill" you. That is why you should take easy days—and sometimes easy weeks or months—to allow your body to rest. I usually refer to this as "periodization" of workouts. Basically, periodization is changing the intensity of your training program by time periods. For example: hard days followed by easy days, to ensure recovery. Periodization is important in any form of physical training.

In addition to allowing for periodization of workouts, you should control the intensity at which you perform each individual workout. You can gauge the intensity of your aerobic training by your heart rate (taking your pulse), or subjectively (estimating percentage of maximum effort). Checking your pulse takes the guesswork out of your training, and is relatively easy to do when swimming intervals due to the break at the wall after each repeat. You have a magic number called your "threshold"—the heart rate at which lactic acid begins to build up faster than you can break it down. Your goal is to do the bulk of your training just below that level. A popular formula uses your age to roughly calculate your threshold: $180 -$ your age $=$ threshold. You should be able to sustain your threshold pace for awhile. Do no more than 5 to 10 percent of your training above threshold on your short-interval days. On easy days, go 10 to 20 percent below threshold.

As you can see, great training—the kind that really builds up your body—is the result of controlled stress. Not enough stress and you will not get much benefit. Too much stress and you break down your body, risking injury and illness. Interval training is the best way to control your level of stress and ensure that you keep on target with your goals. Setting up your workout may take a little more effort than simply "swimming laps," but the rewards will be worth the effort—not to mention that intervals add spice and variety to your workout program.

If you are unfamiliar with the terminology of intervals, here is an example. One of the best interval workouts to perform is a set of 100-yard (or meter) swims. The "repeat" or "interval" time refers to how much time elapses between each push-off. If I instruct you to do 5×100 swims on 2:00, you would swim 100 yards five times; the interval time (in this case, 2 minutes) is the time you have for each swim, including swimming time and rest. In this example, if you swim a 1:30 for the 100, you have 30 seconds to rest before pushing off on your next repeat. As you can see, the entire set takes 10 minutes and there are three variables in the interval equation:

Swim length = L
Number of repeats = R
Interval time = T

$$R \times L \text{ on } T$$

In our example, R is 5, L is 100, and T is $2:00-5 \times 100$ on 2:00. For general fitness, select an interval time to allow approximately 30 seconds of rest. Pick a total yardage for your set that is about half of your total workout yardage, since the object is to swim just slightly faster than you would during a long, straight swim. This is where you will access the adaptive properties of the human body. Try, if possible, to do intervals with a friend whose speed is close to yours. This way you will be able to push off on each swim at the same time, take your rest together, and encourage each other. You will be surprised how interval training will enhance your training program.

If you work out three times a week, performing three distinct workouts—in no particular order—will produce the best results:

Short Intervals: 25s, 50s, 75s, and 100s

Intervals: 100s, 200s, 300s, 400s, and 500s

Long Swim: Straight swim of 300-2,000, depending on your ability and fitness level

All of the above distances refer to either yards or meters, depending on the pool.

Each of these workouts should consist of a warm-up, stroke drills, a main set, optional secondary sets, stroke drills, and a cooldown.

Note: Once your body starts to get used to the workouts, it is time to adjust the intervals. By keeping track of your workouts and making necessary adjustments, such as increasing or decreasing the interval or number of repeats, you will avoid swimming in a rut. Continuous repetition of the same items in a workout is an invitation to stagnation. To help I have suggested workouts at the end of this chapter that will keep things interesting for you.

Warm-up

The warm-up is a time to loosen up and make the transition from land to aquatic mammal. Exactly how many laps you should swim, and how intensely you should swim them, is subjective. Generally, swimming 200 to 500 yards or meters at an easy-to-moderate pace will best prepare you for your drills.

Drills

In the drill portion of your workout you should complete at least one basic stroke drill (see chapter 4) and then fill in with the specific drills (including kick drills) that address your flaws (as discovered in chapter 3). Drills need to be done before and after your main set. Before, do 300 to 500 yards or meters of drills. After, 100 to 200 yards or meters of stroke drills is plenty to get you back to top form. Stroke drills help reestablish good technique, since the effort of completing the main set tends to make us lazy and to let us fall back on bad habits.

Main Set

The main set is the heart of your workout. Its purpose is to challenge your muscles and cardiovascular system to improve. It is the physically demanding part of the workout. Although the hard effort will be uncomfortable at times, it will also release endorphins and leave you feeling a little—maybe even more than a little—high. Record your main set times into a log book, preferably a hardbound book. This will allow you to track your progress.

Cooldown

The cooldown lets your body and mind wind down and make the transition from aquatic back to land mammal. If your workout needs to be cut short then cut down your main set: Never skip warm-up, drills, or cooldown.

Live by the phrase: "Train don't strain." Always listen to your body. Sharp pain anywhere is bad, but especially in your joints (usually your shoulder). Temporary muscular discomfort, on the other hand, is good, and should be considered a positive sign: It means your training is progressing well.

■ ■ ■

What follows are templates for the three types of workouts. These are only guidelines; use the alternative workouts described later in this chapter to add variety. If you cannot complete these workouts, simply cut back to a level you can manage. I have seen swimmers go from not being able to do one lap, to doing these workouts, in six months. Take giant baby steps: Add a few more laps each session. The key to long-term success is persistence.

SHORT INTERVAL WORKOUT

1. Warm-Up	200–500, easy pace
2. Drills	3 × 100 drills, basic and specific for you (from chapter 4); 3–5 × 100 kick-on-side drill
3. Main Set	5–10 × 50 on _____
	5–10 × 25 on _____
	200, off-strokes

4. Drills	200, stroke drills
5. Cooldown	200–500, easy swim

INTERVAL WORKOUT

1. Warm-Up	200–500, easy pace
2. Drills	3 × 100 drills, basic and specific for you (from chapter 4); 3–5 × 100 kick-on-side drill
3. Main Set	5 × 100 on _____ (descending)
	3 × 300 on _____
	200, off-strokes (optional)
4. Drills	200, stroke drills
5. Cooldown	200–500, easy swim

LONG-SWIM WORKOUT

1. Warm-Up	200–500, easy pace
2. Drills	3 × 100 drills, basic and specific for you (from chapter 4); 3–5 × 100 kick-on-side drill
3. Main Set	1 × 1,000–2,000, record time
	200, off-strokes
4. Drills	200, stroke drills
5. Cooldown	200–500, easy swim

Note: There is no mention of distances—yards or meters—since you will most likely complete these workouts in a 25- or 50-meter or -yard pool. Pools that are of odd lengths will require some workout changes. If you are stuck in a 20-yard pool, substitute 20 for 25, and 40 for 50; multiples of 100 will work as is.

The table below will provide you with the information you need to fill your interval times into the workout templates. To use this table you simply need your best 50 time. If you do not know your best 50 time, go to the pool, warm up, and time yourself for an all-out 50. Then go to the table and find the row that has your time. If you move across the chart on that row, you will see your interval times.

REPEAT TIME TABLE

50 time	25s	50s	100s	300s
under :30	:30	:45	1:40	5:00
:31—:35	:35	:50	1:50	5:20
:36—:40	:40	:55	2:00	5:40
:41—:45	:45	1:00	2:15	6:00
:46—:55	:50	1:05	2:30	6:30
:51—:55	:55	1:15	2:45	7:00
:56—1:00	1:00	1:25	3:00	7:30
over 1:00	your time	1:45	3:30	8:00

Note: This table works for meters or yards. Just make sure you are consistent—for instance, use a 50-meter time to get interval times for a meter pool (and vice versa for yards). This table can be used for all strokes. However, very rarely do swimmers repeat longer than 200s of butterfly.

ALTERNATIVE WORKOUT SUGGESTIONS—PROVEN WINNERS

The following 10 workouts are main sets that can be substituted into the workout templates. After each description, a note lets you know which workout template the workout fits into.

1. FAST FREDDIE'S FAVORITE

3 × 500 with 30–45 seconds rest.

Note: Fred does them all hard. I feel that they are better done in a descending set. Great for working at threshold to improve mile time. Good pre- , during- , and postseason.

Workout Template: Interval.

2. TARP'S TORTURE (or Drop-off 100s)

6–12 × 100s. Drop the interval by 10 seconds every two 100s. Start with interval 1:10 slower than best 100 time. Set is over when you cannot make interval. Example: If best 100 time is 1:00, first two 100s on 2:10. Next two on 2:00, etc.

Note: Starts out very aerobic and turns anaerobic. Great workout to do one to two weeks before a key event.

Workout Template: Interval.

3. FERRIS'S FOLLY (or Up Down Ladder by 100)

100, 200, 300, 400, 300, 200, 100. Take 15 to 30 seconds between each swim. Negative split 400: Make trip down ladder faster than up.

Note: One of the best workouts to do to learn and improve pacing. Good pre- and during-season workout.

Workout Template: Interval.

4. THE INDICATOR

10 × 100s on 40 seconds slower than best time.

Note: Should be done once every two weeks to see where you are at. Try to hold pace steady or slightly descend.

Workout Template: Interval.

5. FOR LACTIC ACID LOVERS ONLY (or maybe golf would be better)

12 × ½-pool (12.5-yard/meter) sprints with full recovery. These are all-out efforts. 5 × 50s on 45 seconds slower than best time—fast and steady. 5 ×

50s with fins, same as above, descend. 3 × 100s on 4:00—yes, that is full recovery, so guess what? These babies are fast. Keep good technique on last lap.

Note: This workout is perfect 7–10 days before an event, or on a during-season week when not competing. Not a good idea pre- or postseason.

Workout Template: Short Interval.

6. THE INDICATOR II

10 × 200s on 1:00 minute slower than best time.

Note: This workout is a great anaerobic threshold trainer. As such it is good preseason for competitors, and anytime for fitness swimmers. Good to do once a month, charting progress. Try to hold pace steady or descend.

Workout Template: Interval.

7. MEDAL WINNING MEDLEY TRAINING

16 × 50s, four of each stroke in medley order (butterfly, backstroke, breaststroke, and freestyle) on 20–30 seconds rest between each 50. 5 × 200 medleys, on 45–60 seconds rest.

Note: A terrific workout for your off–strokes. For swimmers who only compete in freestyle (yes, you triathletes), try this workout once a week in the off-season and watch your freestyle improve.

Workout Template: Interval.

8. Long Swim with a Twist

1,000 or more yards straight, every fourth length off-stroke.

Note: You can do just about anything every fourth. Examples: drills, fast swimming, easy swimming, etc.

Workout Template: Long Swim.

9. 25/75 Hike!

10 × 75s with 30 seconds rest, steady pace. 20 × 25s, alternate easy/hard, with 30 seconds rest.

Note: Really go for speed on the 25s.

Workout Template: Short Interval.

10. No Frills Intervals

10 × 50/100s on 30 seconds rest and 1:00 rest respectively.

Note: This set, in which you do a 50 followed by a 100, goes by fast.

Workout Template: Interval.

Here is a sample month of training for a three-times-a-week swimmer. If you can swim more, simply add in other workouts from the template and the supplemental list (I have used the numbered workouts in this example). Only main sets are shown. Obviously, you need to include the rest of the template—warm-up, drills, and cooldown—in every practice.

SAMPLE TRAINING MONTH

DAY	WEEK 1	WEEK 2	WEEK 3	WEEK 4
Monday	Long swim	Short interval		Workout #1
Tuesday			Long swim	
Wednesday	Short interval			Short interval*
Thursday		Long swim	Workout #5	
Friday	Interval			Long swim*
Saturday		Interval	Workout #4	
Sunday				RACE DAY!

* These two workouts are close to Sunday's race, so they should be half your usual distance. If you ordinarily do a 2,000 long swim, here do 1,000, and do it easy. The same goes for Wednesday's short intervals: Do half as many, but still do them fast. With the added rest you should feel great and perform great on race day. More on tapering for events in chapter 8.

DISCIPLINE

Now that you have a goal and plan, the final piece of the puzzle is the discipline to carry them out. Indeed, swimming is a sport that demands a certain amount of discipline. It is not a "game" sport—you are alone for a large part of your workout. Some of my friends affectionately refer to swimming as a "single-lane prison."

There are some things you can do to guarantee success. If you compete, enter races even if they are months away. Having made this commitment, you will find yourself making time to get to workouts. Scheduling time to train is important. Write it in your datebook as an unchangeable part of your day. If there is a masters team or group nearby, join up, and let the power and motivation of the others help you. The last word on discipline is *balance*. Every once in awhile skip a workout and relax. Remember that rest (physical and mental) is as important as training.

■ ■ ■

The ideas I have presented in this chapter are like a great recipe. Follow this tried-and-true plan and reap the benefits.

8

PRACTICAL
SWIMMING TIPS

MAKING THE PLUNGE

One of the biggest hurdles to swimming regularly is the apprehension we all experience at the thought of getting into that wet environment, of making these first few laps when the whole body seems to be saying "get out." Even when the weather is warm, pool water is always chilly relative to our 98.6-degree F (35.3-degree C) core temperature. It does not seem to matter that we always feel better after working out; we want to avoid the shock to our systems that submerging the body in water produces. The only sensible way to approach this fear is to focus on how good you will feel after your swim. Picture this in your mind and chances are you will be more apt to get to the pool and swim. Remember, the water never gets any warmer while you procrastinate over getting into it. As a matter of fact, the sooner you get in, the sooner you will take that nice warm shower.

CROWDED POOLS

When swimming in a crowded pool, try to join swimmers who most closely match your ability. The most effective way to get many swimmers into one lane is to circle swim: go down one side of the lane and come back on the other. The problem with this is that all the swimmers must be swimming at close to the same pace. This is rarely the case at pools where lap swimming is open to all. If you can convince a few friends who are close to you in speed to work out with you and try circle swimming, you will "own" the

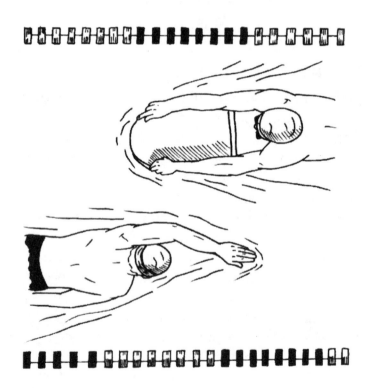

Circle swimming

lane. Another option is to share a lane—two swimmers side by side—the only problem being that the saturation point of the pool is the number of lanes times two swimmers per lane. The bottom line is to try to swim when the pool is not crowded. When all else fails, be a little patient: Someone is usually at the end of his or her swim. Use the extra time to stretch and refocus on your goals.

TO COMPETE OR NOT?

There are many positive aspects to competing; it is, however, by no means mandatory to a successful swimming or exercise program. When I talk about competition with some people they get very apprehensive and bring a lot of negative listening to the conversation. If you too hear a little voice in your head saying things like:

"I hate competition!"

"I'm not competitive!"

"I don't like people who compete!"

"I can't handle the stress!"

"Competition makes me nervous and upset!"

I would ask you to consider the following:

1. Competition takes many forms. You can compete against yourself or the clock if you choose to look at it that way.

2. Competition is a great opportunity to learn what makes you tick. Who knows—learning to enjoy

friendly competition may help you get that job you want, or the man/woman of your dreams!

3. People who enjoy competition view it as a chance to see the rewards of their efforts.

4. Competition can be used as a motivational tool. Notice I said "used." It should never use you. When you say things like: "If I don't beat so-and-so today I'll quit!" then competition is using you. Scheduling yourself to compete in a race, however, definitely helps motivate you to stick with your program.

5. Above all, if you find that competition takes away from your enjoyment of life or the sport, don't do it!

There is so much more to competition than athletic skill. The truly great athlete integrates mind and body. Small improvements are stacked up over time. Did you know that many world class athletes had to overcome severe handicaps and setbacks? Many times a setback is a blessing in disguise: It affords the athlete the opportunity to correct a flaw and end up better than before. The Chinese symbols for crisis and opportunity are one and the same. We just do not see the opportunity as quickly as we would like to. I need to constantly remind myself of this.

COMPETITION: GETTING STARTED

If you are college-age or younger, one or more of three main types of pure swimming competition is open to you:

USS, high school, and college. "USS" stands for "United States Swimming" and is the governing body for competitive-age-group and senior-level national competition. Many high school and college swimmers compete in the off-season in USS meets, since most USS programs are year-round. High school and college swimming events are the same as those in USS, but more emphasis is placed on team scoring. Due to the discipline that swimming requires, many age-group swimmers are also great students and eligible for scholarships at the best colleges in the country.

Although adults can and do join USS and compete in USS swim meets, they more often opt for masters swimming. Masters swimming can be viewed as age-group swimming for adults. Swimmers come to masters swimming from many backgrounds: Some are former college or even Olympic stars who just cannot get enough; others are people who have never competed in anything and are learning as they go. The meets are neat, because you swim with people who are at close to your own ability. That is the way to get good competition. Swimmers in their 20s can be found duking it out with swimmers in their 40s. The times are sorted out later, and standings within the age groups compiled. Starting at age 20, age groups are defined in increments of 5 years. It is interesting to see swimmers get excited about turning 40 and "aging up." There are masters meets locally, regionally, nationally, and internationally. Participants are generally very social and really have a love for swimming. Most plan on swimming for their entire lives. Masters swim teams are popular, and can make a big difference in your training.

There is one other way to pool race—individually. I want to stress that while the aforementioned organized ways to compete are helpful because of the organization, you always have the option of simply timing yourself. When you think about it, that is what you are doing in the end anyway: racing against yourself and the clock.

COMPETITION TIPS FOR PEAK PERFORMANCE

- Rest and tone down your training (tapering) in direct proportion to the importance of the meet. The bigger the event, the longer the taper, and more rest you should take. Put extra time aside one to two weeks before the meet to practice starts and turns. For really big races, shave down, and see what the nubile sensation can do for your swimming. When a swimmer proclaims, "I'm shaved and tapered," watch out—he or she is usually ready for a fast swim. If you are shaving for the first time, be careful. The first time I shaved my legs I ran the razor straight over my shin. A piece of skin came off like a carrot peel—it was not pretty. If you are hairy, use clippers before applying shaving cream and razor. The shaving-down process works for two reasons: It reduces drag, since hair is gone; and then there is the tingling sensation of taking off the top layer or two of skin.

- Do as much planning for swim meets as possible. If needed, bring sunglasses, hat, and sunscreen to protect yourself from the sun. Bring extra goggles, caps, suits, towels, clothes, and food, since swim meets are often long.

- Because most meets are long, prepare some healthful snacks, meals, and plenty of water. Good snack choices include: bananas, any fruit that agrees with you, energy bars, and energy-replacement drinks. The meet is not the time to experiment with new foods—stick to what works. Experiment only during training.

- Make sure you are familiar with the pool walls (and lanes) for your turns and finishes.

- Study the starter's speed. This tells you whether to anticipate the gun or be more patient.

- Positively visualize the race in 30-second scenarios a couple times a day for the couple weeks leading into it. The more vivid and real you can make your picture, the more effective this process will be. Music can be helpful.

- Take long, deep, and slow breaths to calm down before your event. Concentrate on the outbreath.

- Always cooldown and stretch after competition, to help you recover quickly.

- Review the event(s) and analyze (hopefully with the help of a coach) what went right and where you can make improvements.

RACING STARTS

Diving of any kind is one of the most dangerous activities at the swimming pool. For this reason, never practice diving unsupervised. Make sure the water is deep—the deeper the better—but for racing dives, six feet is usually sufficient. All starts are best worked on under the experienced supervision of a swimming coach.

In pool racing the start is critical, and many times determines the winner—especially in sprint races. The starts for freestyle, butterfly, and breaststroke are the same, except that the breaststroke start can go a little deeper because you will take one kick and one stroke before coming up. I will discuss the backstroke start separately.

For many years it was thought that the best racing dive was one in which the swimmer dives almost completely horizontal. However, about ten years ago, swimmers realized they could get farther out by going higher in the air and diving deeper: Upon entry they "scoop" forward and come up farther ahead than a conventional diver would. There are three basic movements to the scoop dive: takeoff, entry, and extension (scoop). After the extension you glide and begin your stroke—much as you do after a push-off.

TAKE OFF

Although some associations still use their own rules for starts, international competition has fairly consistent rules. You begin at a standing position in the middle of the starting block. When the starter says "take your mark," step forward and curl your toes over the end of the block.

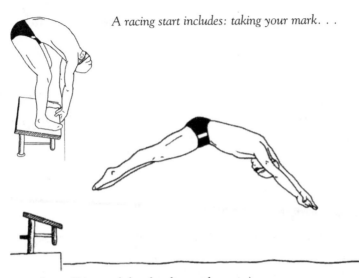

A racing start includes: taking your mark. . .

. . .taking off (up and then bending at the waist). . .

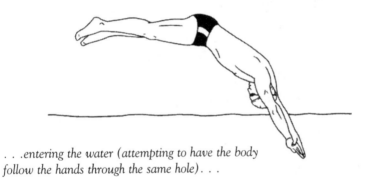

. . .entering the water (attempting to have the body follow the hands through the same hole). . .

. . .and an extension, or "scoop," in the water.

Bend at your waist and wait. At the gun (sometimes a beep), spring up and out.

ENTRY

The objective on entry is to have your hands and feet pierce the same imaginary hole in the water. This means using a slightly piked position.

EXTENSION (SCOOP)

The objective of the scoop is to translate your stored energy (coiled-up body position) into forward thrust. As you enter the water, straighten out (extend) your body and be as streamlined as possible. The conclusion of this move-ment is very much like the glide in the push-off. At this point, begin swimming.

THE BACKSTROKE START

Backstrokers start from a different position: with their feet (heels are required) in the water. The phases of the start are the same: take off, entry, and extension. Do a backward dolphin kick under the water for speed, and to help you reach the surface.

OPEN-WATER SWIMMING TIPS

- All of the competition tips for peak perfor-mance—with the exception of starts and turns —apply here.

- Always choose a bright-colored cap. When the water is below 65 degrees F (18 degrees C) I suggest wearing a neoprene cap for extra warmth; wear the bright latex cap over the neoprene one.

- If the swim heads into a rising sun (not uncommon), be sure to use smoke-tinted or mirrored goggles to help you see. Sometimes the sun is so glaring that you need to flip onto your back and see where you have come from to help you figure out where to go.

- Do some head-up swimming (described in chapter 4) in workouts to prepare for sighting buoys. Practice breaststroke and backstroke as well; they, too, can come in handy when you are searching for course markers. When the water is very choppy, breaststroke can help you navigate; and it is a way to take a rest from freestyle if you need one.

- If you are using a wet suit, use a lubricant (silicone spray works best; do not use Vaseline) on your neck and shoulder areas. For a triathlon put some on your calves to facilitate a quick change of clothes.

- Know the course. Swim it a day or two ahead of time if possible. On race day, analyze the course before you swim to pick the best starting position—the one that allows you to swim the shortest possible line. Watch the other athletes warm up as well; notice if they are swept to one side or the other. This information will be invaluable when you decide where to enter the water. It will also show you if course conditions have changed since the day before. It is not uncommon to have the sweep or current change direction overnight.

- Use the flip-on-the-back technique for cornering buoys quickly. This technique is easy to master with a little practice. Approach the buoy and turn onto your back, toward the buoy. Continue to roll over, onto your stomach, and pivot 90 degrees. In this way you can maintain speed and save time.

- Practice drafting in the pool while circle swimming. This will help when you get in the open water. Make sure the swimmer you are following is swimming a straight line. Do not go on blind faith.

- Play water polo at every opportunity. This is the best way to prepare for the physicality of open-water swimming. Yes, open-water swimming is, at least sometimes, a contact sport. Put goggles on beneath your cap so that, if they get knocked off your face, you can put them back on. If you do get hit, do a little easy breaststroke to catch your breath, then—if you are not hurt—continue.

- Do not start up front unless you belong there— you will get hit! Seed yourself appropriately. If you are timid, take an outside line. You may end up swimming a little more, but getting clocked can put you out of the race.

- Pacing: Start off at a moderate pace (unless you are going for a lead spot) and build into your swim. Push the pace between one-third and two-thirds of the way into the race. For a triathlon, back off your pace slightly toward the end, to start visualizing the transition to biking.

- Practice by taking some longer swim sets out fast, to simulate swimming for a good line around buoys. This will teach you to tolerate high lactic acid and then settle into a pace.

- Learn to sprint well so you can "pack jump"— sprint from one pack of swimmers to another, stay in their draft for awhile, and move on.

- Practice bilateral breathing so you can see on both sides of yourself without stopping.

- Practice shoreline entries by dolphining: running and diving repeatedly until the water is too deep.

- For triathlons, be sure to practice negative splitting your swims; this will help you feel strong at the end of the swim segment.

TRIATHLON SWIMMING - RACE DAY TIPS

Try to get a good sleep two nights before a race since you

are generally a little less pumped up then. See if you can finish all work and responsibilities so as to have a clear mind. Pack a race bag early—preferably the night before—using a check list. You can start with this one and add your own personal items.

CHECKLIST

race numbers

magic marker

suit

goggles

cap

towel

wet suit

lubricant

bike

helmet

cycling shoes

cycling clothes (optional—many triathletes race in their swimsuits)

running shoes and socks

running clothes (optional—many triathletes race in their swimsuits)

floor pump

    water pan (to rinse feet after swim)

    water bottles

    energy food (if long race)

After going over your checklist the night before, try to get some rest. When I raced the Hawaii Ironman, I can remember staring at the ceiling all night. I was not concerned, since I did not expect any sleep—just some rest for the body.

Because of the prerace anxiety factor, it is usually not a problem getting up early on race morning. That is a good thing, since you need to eat a little something—the earlier the better. Try to eat one-and-a-half to three hours before the event. The quantity depends on the duration of the race. If the race will be less than two hours long, eat lightly—perhaps a piece of toast or an energy bar and water. If it will be more than two hours long, eat a more substantial meal such as oatmeal and juice. Use what works for you and never, ever try something new on race day. Triathletes call that a rookie mistake. That goes for new anything, too: food, sneakers, bike, clothes, and so on. No matter what, drink lots of water. Get to the race site early and lay out your gear. Gain confidence from knowing you have done your training and preparation for competition.

9

FLEXIBILITY
TRAINING

Flexibility is an often overlooked aspect of fitness and performance. Through the course of normal living, muscles shorten. Little by little as you age you lose your range of motion. You can also lose range of motion from injuries and muscle overuse. When you see someone who exudes health and youth, it may not be obvious, but flexibility is at the core of what you see. Someone hunched over and taking small steps (basically, someone who is inflexible) does not look, act, or feel vibrant and healthy. The good news is that flexibility and hence range of motion can be restored and improved by stretching.

My flexibility research and training led me to meet and work with Aaron Mattes, who pioneered Active Isolated (AI) Stretching. I have found his methods more useful, effective, and enjoyable than all other forms of stretching. He has written an excellent book entitled *Active and*

Assistive Isolated Stretching that I urge you to not only buy, but use. In it he covers the entire body—much more than I could possibly do in this single chapter.

This chapter will serve as an introduction to AI stretching, briefly covering the principles and practices of shoulder flexibility. The range of motion of the shoulder is very important to swimming. Good to excellent range of motion will lead to longer, more efficient strokes. Shoulder stretching is an integral part of shoulder rehabilitation and injury prevention. Your neck, hips, legs, and trunk are also very important and should be addressed as well.

Stretching exercises have progressed from ballistic, to static, to active isolated. "Ballistic stretching" involves using jerking movements to go beyond a certain point in the stretch. It has all but been abandoned, as it puts tremendous stress on muscles and tendons and can cause injury. "Static stretching" is a gentler approach: You stretch slowly beyond what is comfortable and hold it for 20, 30, 60 seconds or longer. Although this method is popular, it ignores a very basic principle of muscle physiology, the stretch reflex. To protect itself, the body responds (in approximately two seconds) to stretching by contracting the very muscle you are attempting to stretch. So with static stretching you end up fighting yourself and engaging in a kind of tug-of-war.

Active isolated stretching has three great advantages— they are actually the principles on which it is based:

1. You contract not the targeted muscle, but its opposing muscle(s); this has the physiological effect of relaxing the muscle you wish to stretch.

2. You hold the stretch for only two seconds, there-fore never engaging the stretch reflex.

3. You repeat the movement 8 to 10 times. This allows you to go farther with every repeat. This also has the effect of bathing your muscles in fresh blood. When done properly, AI Stretching speeds healing and recovery due to this influx of fresh blood (nutrients). Concentrating on breathing out throughout the stretches enhances this flush-ing and oxygenation of the tissue. This is why AI Stretching is as or more effective than massage for recovery.

These advantages also describe the basic technique of AI Stretching. All that is left is for you to learn its movements and follow its principles. I can only show you some of its key movements, for the shoulders, again, I encourage you to get Aaron Mattes's book, and to do as much AI Stretching as you can.

ARM CIRCLES (CIRCUMDUCTION)

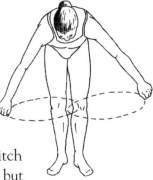

Bend at your waist and swing your arms in opposing circles (i.e., your right arm counter-clockwise, your left arm clock-wise). Do 10 swings then switch directions. This is not a stretch, but an exercise to warm up (increase blood flow to) the shoulders.

Arm circles to warm up the shoulder area

ARMS OUT TO SIDE AND BACK (HORIZONTAL ABDUCTION)

Standing straight, preferably facing a mirror, bring your arms out and back. Hold at this stretched position for two seconds and repeat 10 times. Bring your arms a little higher and farther back on each repetition. This stretches your chest.

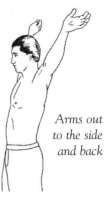

Arms out to the side and back

ARMS UP BEHIND (HYPEREXTENSION)

Standing straight, preferably facing a mirror, bring your arms up behind your body. Hold at this stretched position for two seconds and repeat 10 times. This stretches your biceps and the fronts of your shoulders.

Arms up behind you

EXTERNAL ROTATION

Standing straight, preferably facing a mirror, lift your arms out to the side with 90-degree bends in your elbows. Rotate your shoulders backward. Hold at this stretched position for two seconds and repeat 10 times. This stretches the internal rotators of your shoulders.

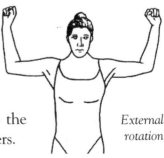

External rotation

INTERNAL ROTATION

Standing straight, preferably facing a mirror, lift your arms out to your sides with 90-degree bends in your elbows. Rotate your shoulders foreward. Hold at this stretched position for two seconds and repeat 10 times. This stretches the external rotators of your shoulders.

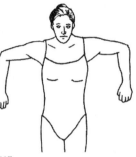

Internal rotation

ARM ACROSS CHEST (HORIZONTAL FLEXION)

Standing straight, preferably facing a mirror, bring one arm across your body. Assist at the end with your other hand. Hold at this stretched position for two seconds and repeat 10 times. This stretches your rotator cuff.

Arm across chest, keeping shoulder down

ARM ACROSS CHEST, HAND OVER BACK (HORIZONTAL FLEXION)

This is a slight variation on the arm-across-the-chest stretch. Standing straight, preferably facing a mirror, bring one arm across your body. Drop the hand over your shoulder and crawl your fingers down your back. Assist at the end with your other hand. Hold at this

Arm across chest, crawling hand over back

stretched position for two seconds and repeat 10 times. This stretches your rotator cuff.

TRICEPS STRETCH

Although this is technically not a shoulder stretch, it is important for shoulder flexibility. Standing straight, preferably facing a mirror, bring one arm up and back with your elbow bent. Assist at the end with your other hand. Hold at this stretched position for two seconds and repeat 10 times. This stretches your triceps.

Elbow back to stretch the triceps

HANDCLASP BEHIND (POSTERIOR HANDCLASP)

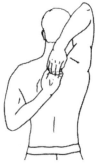

Standing straight, preferably facing a mirror, try to clasp hand in each direction. If you cannot, simply use a rope and inch your hands toward each other. Hold at this stretched position for two seconds and repeat 10 times. *Note:* These exercises are to be done without pain. Any pain may indicate an injury and should be treated by a health care professional.

Hands clasped behind you

■ ■ ■

Performing these stretches before and after a swim session will improve your swimming and recovery. Again I urge you to investigate this method for your entire body and enjoy the benefits of total flexibility. The more I work with people, the more I see flexibility as the foundation of health and fitness.

10

STRENGTH TRAINING

A strength training program—like a stretching program—should address the entire body. More research every year extols the health benefits of strength conditioning (sometimes referred to as "weight training"). I can tell you from my experience as a personal trainer that strength training is one of the cornerstones of health. It helps prevent osteoporosis, increase confidence, and improve performance. Strength training is for all ages—especially the older population. Children (including young adults) should not lift heavy weights, because their bones are still growing. They should concentrate more on strengthening exercises that use their body weight for resistance: push-ups, pull-ups, and dips.

Two exercises hone in on swimming's prime movers: lat pull-downs and dips. These exercises strengthen the latissimus dorsi and triceps muscles, respectively—which are both important for a powerful pull. To maximize the benefit of working these specific muscles, balance their increasing strength by training the rest of your body's muscles as well.

As I have mentioned several times, the shoulder is the swimmer's Achilles' heel. Poor technique, poor flexibility, and lack of strength can add to its vulnerability. Unlike the hip, the shoulder is not held in place completely by its structure. The shoulder (technically, the glenohumeral joint) is reinforced by active muscle support. Four muscles form a musculotendinous cuff around the joint (since two of these are rotators, these muscles are often collectively referred to as the "rotator cuff"): the supraspinatus, infraspinatus fascia, teres minor, and subscapularis. You could refer to these as the "intrinsic" muscles of the shoulder. When these are all flexible and strong, the shoulder has many arm movers, and this provides almost unlimited mobility.

Since these muscles are so important, I suggest you perform the following routine even if you do no other weight training. The weights are light, and you do not need a gym. There are even more cuff exercises than I can show you here. If this is a problem area for you, consult a physician and find a good therapist to work with—one who has successful experience in this area.

ROUTINE FOR ROTATOR CUFF (INTRINSIC SHOULDER MUSCLES)

These exercises are to be done with light weights. Some athletes start with one or no pounds of resistance! That is fine; you will be doing 5 to 10 pounds soon enough. Concentrate on your form and breathing.

Correct pacing and breathing for this and all strength training is as follows: On the positive movement (lifting or pushing the weight), breathe out. Do this positive movement to a two count. On the negative (bringing the weight back), breathe in. Do the negative to a four count. The negative movement is where much of the strength is gained.

EXERCISE	BRIEF DESCRIPTION
Lateral raise	Seated or standing, and preferably facing a mirror, raise your arms out to your sides to shoulder height.
Posterior raise	Seated or standing, and preferably facing a mirror, raise your arms behind you as high as you can.
Anterior raise	Seated or standing, and preferably facing a mirror, raise your arms in front of you to shoulder height.
Internal rotators	Lying on your side, and using your bottom arm, rotate your shoulder internally (bring your hand to your chest). Flip to your other side and repeat with your other shoulder.
External rotators	Lying on your side, and using your top arm, rotate your shoulder externally (bring your hand away from your body). Flip to your other side and repeat with your other shoulder.
Shoulder shrug	Seated or standing, and preferably facing a mirror, shrug your shoulders forward in a circular motion. Repeat the shrug movement in reverse.

As you can see, these exercises can easily be done while watching the news or conversing with your family. That is right: No excuses. I have seen way too many swimmers needlessly sidelined because they neglected these muscles.

To increase strength in muscles you need to work them two to three times per week. Do 1 to 3 sets of each exercise, with 10 to 15 repetitions in each set. When you can easily achieve 15 reps in good form, it is time to increase resistance by 5 to 10 percent. For exercises like push-ups that use your own weight, simply keep increasing reps in good form. As in swimming, technique is the most important part of strength training. It does not matter how much weight you can lift if you are doing so by jerking it or using momentum or other muscles.

SPECIFICITY

The swim bench is a very efficient and effective strength training device for swimmers, because it utilizes the specificity principle—with it you use your muscles in the same way you do while swimming. Resistance swim benches are available for $300 to $800. Making your own device with surgical tubing is effective and will probably cost you less than $10. In many ways, surgical tubing devices are superior to the expensive swim trainers. With surgical tubing, resistance increases as you get farther into the pull. This promotes the "soft in front, accelerate at the end" stroke I discussed in chapter 2. (See appendix B for instructions on how to make your own swim trainer.)

Whether you make your own swim trainer or buy one, the principle behind its use is the same. It is a departure from standard strength conditioning, which isolates the muscles. For overall body-strength balance, isolation is the way to go. For movement specificity and time saving, though, specificity training wins. My suggestion is a little of both.

SUGGESTED STRENGTH TRAINING PROGRAM FOR SWIMMERS

- First, begin with a complete stretching routine (see chapter 9).

- Second, strengthen your intrinsic shoulder muscles by completing the rotator cuff routine (see pages 128–130).

- Third, for specificity training, complete 3 sets (30 reps each) of swim-bench movements, each set consisting of the elbow flexion and pull phases of your arm cycle. Your stroke mechanics are the target of this exercise at first; later, you can focus on intensity. (See appendix B.)

- Finally, the following exercises can be done at a gym with free weights and or machines. If you are unfamiliar with weight training, consult a book (see appendix C) or have a personal trainer or physical therapist show you what to do.

Note: Whenever possible use free weights and work your limbs separately. The reasons are that this helps you work your balance and frees your range of motion without getting compensation from your stronger side. Keep a log. Alternate hard and easy days (periodization). A good way

EXERCISE	MUSCLES	TYPE OF EQUIPMENT
1. Squats	Gluteals, quads	machine or free weights
2. Leg extension	Quads	machine
3. Leg curl	Hamstrings	machine
4. Calf raises	Calf group	machine
5. Lat pull-down	Lats	machine or free weights
6. Push-ups	Chest	none needed
7. Dips	Triceps, deltoids	machine
8. Pull-ups	Arms, shoulders, back	back machine
9. Shoulder press	Deltoids	machine or free weights
10. Biceps curl	Biceps	machine or free weights
11. Triceps extension	Triceps	machine or free weights
12. Crunches (knees at 90 degrees)	Abdominal	none needed
13. Reverse sit-up	Abdominal	none needed
14. Hyperextensions	Lower back	none needed
15. Trunk twists, 100—200	Lower back	none needed or free weights

to get started on a program like this is to join a well-equipped gym and have a session or two with a trainer to get oriented on the equipment.

■　■　■

Although strength training is an optional part of your training program, it pays big dividends on the time you invest. It is also good for your ego when you start seeing new muscle definition. I know many swimmers, including myself, who will skip a swim practice before missing a weight session. There truly is a high from "pumping." Many people fear that lifting weights will make them look like bodybuilders. Worry not. Bodybuilders lift weights four hours a day, six days a week, and take special supplements. They also do some sets of one or two reps with heavy weights, in order to really tear down the muscle so it will rebuild much larger. With the help of a trainer, try the program described in this chapter instead. Feel the power in your body and see the definition.

11

NUTRITION

Garbage in, garbage out.

Proper food selection, hydration, and meal timing are crucial to good health and optimum performance. Together, they can enhance your athletic competitiveness by providing you the fuels necessary for energy and for tissue development and repair.

There is certainly no shortage of nutritional information available—guidebooks and videos line store shelves. With so much information, selecting a healthy diet can be confusing. Not only are there many choices, but each person's needs are different. Some have food allergies or sensitivities that need to be addressed. In addition, stress can change our bodies' needs. It is my belief that no one program or ratio of fat to carbohydrate to protein is ideal for everyone all the time. Having said this, I can give you some guidelines that I have found helpful not only to my athletic pursuits, but also to those of the many clients and athletes I work with.

WHAT?

Imagine you own a brand new Ferrari. What type of fuel would you put in it? I imagine the best available. How much fuel would you put in it? Anywhere from part-fill to fill, right? But it is harder to tell when you are full, for a few reasons. Your tank can expand, allowing you to overfill. Also, there is a lag between the time you are physically full, and the time you "feel" full. I think your body is more important than a car, don't you agree?

The more you incorporate whole, unprocessed foods into your diet, the better you will feel and perform. And the higher the water content, the better the food. Fruits and vegetables are key. It is helpful to juice some of them, as this process yields a more concentrated source of vitamins and minerals. You should also emphasize whole grain cereals and breads in your diet, because these foods provide carbohydrate calories to fuel your muscle and brain tissues (after all, swimming is the thinking person's sport). Refrain from or limit consumption of meat, saturated fat, coffee, alcohol, and refined sugar. The evidence that these substances contribute to disease mounts. You do need some fat—you should see the no-fat-diet fad coming to an end shortly—for hormone production, and to lubricate your organs. However, consume only high-quality fats, like olive and other vegetable oils, avocados, and so on. A little fat (15 to 30 percent of your diet) will help you sustain a higher energy level.

Staying well hydrated is as or more important than selecting the correct foods. Drink plenty of fluids, especially water. Water makes up the largest percentage of the body and is involved in almost all its processes—stabilizing body temperature, transporting nutrients, converting fat to usable energy, and so on. Inadequate fluid intake reduces your body's ability to perform these tasks, and limits your ability to achieve your potential.

Supplements can be helpful but should, I feel, be prescribed by an experienced professional. Some personal trainers are well trained in nutrition, but a better choice is a sports nutritionist or chiropractor. Try to work with someone who does not sell vitamins; salespeople tend to be biased. My personal supplement recommendation is a powdered multiple vitamin-mineral combo. Powder can be mixed with juice to provide the most effective way to take supplements: Your body does not have to break down a pill, and receives the benefit of additional fluid intake.

WHEN?

You are going on a car trip. Do you fill up with fuel before you go, or after you have driven 500 miles? Seems simple, yet we frequently run on empty all day and fill up before going to bed. Then we wonder why we performed poorly, had no energy, were irritable, slept poorly, and had trouble staying awake during the day. I believe this creates unnecessary suffering and stress in our lives.

When you eat can be as important as what you eat. Eat a hearty breakfast first thing or, if your schedule includes an early-morning workout, as soon after it as possible. Try breaking up meals and doing what animals do—grazing. Nutritionists are starting to see the benefits of several smaller meals spaced out through the day. Snacking on fruits and vegetables between meals is a great way to get vitamins, minerals, and energy. Eat lightly at dinner, and not too late—just as our bodies are winding down and preparing to rest, we don't want to overload them with the hard work of digesting big meals. For those trying to lose weight, eating late is dietary suicide. More calories are stored as fat if eaten at night than earlier.

If you are someone who frequently runs on empty and or dumps coffee, soda, cookies, or muffins into yourself to keep going, I want to give you a 7-day challenge. Are you up for it? Commit to eating a healthy breakfast and lunch, snacking on fruits and veggies between meals, and having a light dinner for seven days. My belief is you will feel better than you can imagine—it just may change your life. I think you are more valuable than a Ferrari, but it does not matter what I think. What do you think? Go for it. Of course, if you do intense workouts in the evening from seven to nine, you need to eat a little more later in the day. Just be sure you do not start your workout on empty and follow it with a two-hour raid on the fridge. I know from experience that this is counterproductive.

Keep healthy snacks handy in case you have to delay or miss a meal. Snacks like fruit, bottled water, nuts and seeds, and energy bars are ideal. But try to not skip meals.

Proper nutrition is a personal and subjective subject. Try some of the ideas here. Read some of the books listed. Find people who are getting results. Then listen to your own body and mind, and develop eating habits that serve you.

12

CROSS
TRAINING

I n case you have not noticed, I love swimming! However, swimming is not the answer to everything. It is not "the only exercise I need." Certainly it is an awesome form of aerobic exercise. And, while it is arguably the best all-around exercise, it does fall short in a few areas. One is the strengthening of bones. Bones only come to maintain strength from weight-bearing exercise such as weight training and running. As I noted in chapter 10, more and more studies show the benefits of weight training in maintaining a strong frame and preventing and treating osteoporosis.

Another area in which swimming falls short is weight loss. Swimming is not the best way to maintain or lose weight. There are a few reasons for this. Being in the water cools the body and lowers calorie consumption. Lying horizontally does not work the heart as hard as forcing it to pump against gravity—as in running, for example. Lastly, the body adapts to being in water by promoting a subcutaneous layer of fat for buoyancy and protection (especially if the water is cold). Please do not allow this information to make you consider abandoning swimming. If losing weight is a concern of yours then supplement swimming with running, cycling, stair climbing, or another aerobic activity. There are two important variables to calorie consumption: the duration and the intensity of activity. Duration is how long you excercise; it should range from 30 to 60 minutes. Always use a heart rate monitor to measure the intensity of your excercise. Train in your target range. Letting your heart rate drop below your target range for more than a couple minutes greatly reduces excercise's benefit. Target range is defined as 60 to 75 percent of your maximum heart rate (the experts are still not sure exactly, but I have had great results with my clients using 70 percent). As an example, if you go to a cardiologist for a stress test (which I insist on for clients over 40 who are just starting a program) and he or she says your max is 170, your target is then 119. The effect we like from aerobic training is increased metabolism and calorie consumption. The synergistic effect of swimming and other activities holds the key to lifelong health and fitness. Cross training gets you the best of everything and also keeps you from getting bored.

Exercise in general, and swimming specifically, is one of the three points that make up what I refer to as the "health triad": mind (attitude, spirituality), body (exercise), and diet. Balance of these three areas is the art of healthy living.

"The Beauty is in the Balance."

GLOSSARY

Adduction – Adduction is the movement of a limb toward the body (i.e. the pull phase of the arm cycle).

Catch – Combination of elbow flexion and medial rotation of shoulder.

Descending – Descending is when each successive swim in a set is faster than the one before.

Dolphining – Dolphining is a technique for entering the water from the shoreline, whereby a swimmer repeatedly runs, jumps, and dives into the water until the water is too deep, at which point he or she starts swimming.

Drafting – Drafting is the act of swimming close enough to the swimmer in front of you, that he or she is overcoming much of the water's resistance. You can save 20 to 30 percent of your energy by drafting.

Drag – Drag is pressure opposing a swimmer's forward motion. There are a number of ways for a swimmer to minimize drag: wear a nylon or lycra swimsuit, wear a swim cap, shave body hair, and stay as streamlined as possible.

Elbow flexion – Elbow flexion is the act whereby a swimmer bends his or her elbow, underwater, to create a large pulling surface for the pull phase of the arm cycle. It is not a powerful movement, but it is essential to the powerful pull phase of each stroke. See medial rotation.

Feel for the water – "Feel for the water" is the sense or instinct of searching out still water for forward propulsion. A swimmer can generate more force pushing against still water, as opposed to water that is already moving.

High elbow – High elbow, during the pull phase of the arm cycle, is crucial for all the strokes, and is the result of good elbow flexion.

Interval – An interval is a workout that has three variables: swim length, number of repeats, and an interval time. For example, a coach may ask you to swim 100 meters of freestyle, 5 times, starting each 100 meters every 2 minutes: 5 × 100 on 2. If it takes you 1:45 to complete a 100 meter freestyle, then you have 15 seconds of rest before the next swim.

Lap/length – In all sports one lap is equal to one "round trip." In swimming this equals two pool lengths, even though many coaches really mean one length when they say one lap.

Lift – Lift is a force created at a 90-degree angle to drag (i.e. the force that gets—and keeps—planes in the air). In swimming, lift helps keep the body up and moving forward.

Long axis rotation – Long axis rotation is a rotation, of the entire body, along an imaginary line up the spine and out the top of a swimmer's head. This is sometimes referred to as the body roll.

Long course – All international swim meets, including the Olympics, are contested in a 50 meter pool, usually referred to as long course.

Main set – The main set is the set in the middle of a swimmer's workout, which requires the most effort, and which usually consists of sprints, intervals, or a long swim.

Medial rotation – Medial rotation is the rotation of a joint toward the midline. When the hand and arm are over the head, medial rotation of the shoulder actually moves the arm and hand out. Combines with elbow flexion in the "catch."

Negative split – A negative split is when a swimmer makes the second half of the swim faster than the first half.

Personal record – Personal record is a swimmer's best time for a particular event, often called a P.R.

Rhythm – When a swimmer achieves good timing between pull, kick, and rotation, there is usually a synergistic effect that causes his or her swimming to feel rhythmic and almost as if it is self-propelling.

S-shaped pull pattern – The S-pull pattern is the pattern made, when viewed from below, during the pull phase of the arm cycle. Many good swimmers use this technique to maximize the benefits of sculling, and of pulling against still water as opposed to water that is already moving.

Sculling – Sculling is the act of moving a limb back and forth to create force at a 90-degree angle. It explains why, in every stroke, a swimmer does not simply pull straight back, but instead forms an S-shaped pull pattern, and why the kick is an up-and-down movement that creates forward propulsion.

Set – A set is a series of swims that make up a portion of a workout, the main set, for example.

Short course – High school and college swim meets are contested in the more common, 25 yard or meter pool, usually referred to as short course.

Shoulder elevation – Shoulder elevation is the lifting of the shoulder girdle (a forward movement from the horizontal swimming position), which is very important for getting the maximum stroke extension.

Slipstream – Imagine the lines formed when water makes contact with a swimmer's body and slides around it. These lines (streams) form the slipstream. To minimize drag, the only movements that should occur outside of the slipstream are ones that help move a swimmer forward (like pulling and kicking).

Streamline – Streamline is the sleek, aquadynamic body position desired by all swimmers to minimize drag.

Tapering – Tapering is the act whereby an athlete gradually reduces the intensity and duration of his or her workouts, to prepare for a meet or competition.

SWIMMING
INJURIES

SWIMMER'S EAR

Some swimmers have a problem releasing the water from the ear canal after a swim. Alcohol on a cotton swab can help. If the problem persists, see a doctor, and consider using a pair of molded ear plugs.

SHOULDER PAIN

First of all make 100 percent sure your stroke is correct. A poor stroke can create shoulder problems. If pain is acute you will need to take a break from swimming and see a sports specialist immediately. Ice, massage, and stretching and strengthening can usually do the trick for simple tendonitis. Again, check with a specialist if your pain does not subside.

DIRECTIONS FOR
MAKING A SWIM BENCH[*]

WHAT YOU NEED

- Purchase 6 feet of ¼-inch surgical tubing from a surgical supply company.

- Purchase a package of nylon ties from a hardware store or bicycle shop.

- Purchase a foot of ¼-inch nylon rope and cut into two 6-inch pieces.

- Use a pair of swimming paddles or cut two Plexiglass (¼-inch-thick) paddles, 4 inches by 6 inches each.

WHAT TO DO

- Drill ¼-inch holes 2 inches down and ¾ inch in on the paddles (two holes, one in each side of the paddle). Tie a knot in the 6-inch rope and slip it through one of the holes. Slip the other end through the other hole and tie another knot. Repeat with the other paddle.

- Take the 6-foot piece of tubing and attach each end to a paddle by overlapping an inch of tubing in the middle of the loop of rope, and securing with a nylon tie.

HOW TO USE YOUR NEW TRAINER

Get a weight-lifting-type bench and put one end on a 6- to 12-inch object (for instance, a block of wood). This will allow you to lie on your stomach with your head higher than your feet. Find a secure, vertical object around which to put your tubing-paddle combination. (If you cannot get a bench, lean over at the waist to simulate lying down; this works well on the pool deck, with a ladder as the stationary object.) Situate yourself far enough away from the pole so that there is no slack in the tubing when your arms are outstretched in front. Perform sets of elbow flexion and pull (adduction) movements, concentrating on form. Go slowly at the beginning of each movement, and accelerate as you pull back. Make sure your first movement is to bend your elbow—this maximizes lat involvement. Do three sets of 30 each (elbow flexion and pull [adduction]) in good form and increase the reps to reach 100. As you progress you can move farther away, which increases the resistance. On the trainer it is easy to see if your technique is correct. See chapter 2 to review elbow flexion and the pull phases of the arm cycle. This form of strength training is highly effective because you are working on technique and strength at the same time. As with all strength training, allow at least 48 hours between sessions to make sure your muscles recover. Strength training causes microtears in your muscles and they need time to repair. Stressing them again without this 48-hour recovery time can weaken them.

*Warning: Use extreme caution when using surgical tubing and tethers. Since there is the possibility of the tubes snapping, wear eye protection and inspect the tubing before and after every use.

SUGGESTED READING

BOOKS

Balch, James, M.D. and Phyllis Balch, C.N.C. *Nutritional Healing*. Avery Publishing, 1992. A great resource for answering all of your technical questions on nutrition.

Chambliss, Daniel F. *Champions: The Making of Olympic Swimmers*. William Morrow & Company, 1988. An excellent book describing the high level of discipline in world-class swimming. Gives the reader an inside view of the Mission Viejo swimming program and other mega-yardage programs of the '70s and '80s that have led to unbelievable drops in world record times.

Chavoor, Sherman. *The 50-Meter Jungle*. Coward, McCann, Geoghegan, Inc., 1973. Goes behind the scenes of the greatest swimmer of all, Mark Spitz, and what it takes to be a champion.

Counsilman, M.D., James. *The Complete Book of Swimming.* Atheneum, 1979. From the man who brought swimming out of the dark ages with his 1968 book, *The Science of Swimming* (Prentice Hall). "Doc" Counsilman exudes love for swimming in every sentence. Although almost twenty years old, this book has interesting sections on learning to swim and the utility strokes (elementary backstroke and sidestroke).

Fahey, Thomas D. *Basic Weight Training for Men and Women.* Second Edition. Mayfield Publishers, 1993. A good book to show you the various ways to work your muscles using free weights and machines.

Gallagher, Harry. *Harry Gallagher on Swimming.* Pelham Books, 1970. An older book with some terrific history and timeless principles. Harry Gallagher was one of Australia's finest coaches.

Haas, Robert, M.D. *Eat to Win and Eat to Succeed.* Signet 1983, 1986. Some good tips on nutrition and the athlete. Nice approach to achieving balance in terms of diet.

Mattes, Aaron. *Active and Assistive Isolated Stretching.* Published by Aaron Mattes, 2828 Clark Road, Sarrasota, Florida 34231. This is a pioneering book in flexibility and strength training. Aaron's clinic in Florida is a place to consider seeking treatment for injuries and for peak athletic performance.

Ryan, Frank, M.D. *Butterfly Swimming, Backstroke Swimming, and Breaststroke Swimming.* The Viking Press, 1974. Three separate books that are excellent for the beginner. Some of the technique shown is outdated for competition, however the basic principles are all here.

Sprawson, Charles. *Haunts of the Black Masseur: The Swimmer as Hero.* Pantheon Books, 1992. This book explores swimming's ultra-esoteric side. What swimming has been to people of different cultures, with interesting stories of Tennessee Williams' and Scott Fitzgerald's relationship to the water. Very interesting reading.

Whittin, Philip. *The Complete Book of Swimming.* Random House, 1994. An up-to-date book on swimming with a terrific appendix that includes world age-group and masters records.

PUBLICATIONS

Fitness Swimmer
Rodale Press
33 East Minor Street
Emmaus, PA 18049
(610) 967-8281
This publication is devoted to the fitness swimmer.

Inside Triathlon
Inside Communications
1830 North 55th Street
Boulder, CO 80301

(303) 440-0601
An informative triathlon publication with many articles on training.

Swim, Swimming World, and *Swimming Technique*
Sports Publications, Inc.
228 Nevada Street
El Segundo, CA 90245
(310) 607-9956
Three separate magazines published for slightly different audiences; *Swim* is primarily for masters and fitness swimmers, *Swimming World* is for age-group and national-level competitors, and *Swimming Technique* is for coaches and techies.

Swimming Times
Harold Fern House
Derby Square
Loughborough
Leicestershire LE11 0AL
ENGLAND
(01509) 234433

Triathlete Magazine
W. Publishing Group, Inc.
121 Second Street
San Francisco, CA 94105
(415) 777-6939
A glossy triathlon publication published in the United States, France, and Germany.

220 Magazine
Newstead Press
P.O. Box 613
Swindon, SN1 4TA England
(1793) 533713
5835 Avenida Encinas, Suite 127
Carlsbad, CA 92008
(619) 931-1501
A glossy triathlon publication covering England, Europe, and the United States race scene.

CATALOGS

Energetics
1187 Coast Village Road, #1-280
Santa Barbara, CA 93108
(800) 366-5924
A general fitness and health catalog.

The Swim Zone
918 4th Street North
St. Petersburgh, FL 33701
(800) 329-0013
(813) 822-SWIM
A swimwear catalog.

World Wide Aquatics
10500 University Center Drive, Suite 250
Tampa, FL 33612
(800) 726-1530
(813) 972-0818
A swimwear catalog.

ORGANIZATIONS

WITHIN THE UNITED STATES

Tri-Fed
P.O. Box 15820
Colorado Springs, CO 80935
(719) 597-9090
The national governing body for triathlons. Many races require that you be a member.

United States Swimming
1750 East Boulder Street
Colorado Springs, CO 80909
(719) 578-4578
The national governing body for Senior, Age-group, and Olympic swimmers.

US Masters
2nd Peter Avenue
Rutland, MA 01543

(508) 886-6631
The governing body for masters swimming, ages 19 and up.

OUTSIDE THE UNITED STATES

Amateur Swimming Federation of Great Britain (includes Masters)
Harold Fein House
Derby Square
Loughborough, England LE11 OAL
(01509) 230431

Aussie Masters Swim Inc.
P.O. Box 207
Cowan Dilla, Australia SA5033
(08) 3441217

Australia Swimming Inc.
ACT Sports House, Rm. 7
Maitland Street
Hackett, Australia ACT2602
(06) 2573255

Masters National Office
c/o Jackie Spry
Box 526
Elmsdale, Nova Scotia BONIMO
(902) 883-8833

Swimming Canada
1600 James Maismith, Suite 503
Gloucester, Ontario KIB5N4
(613) 748-5673

Now that you have *The Essential Swimmer*, give your swimming the one-two punch by utilizing *Swim Power*, the swimming video that will help you visualize all the concepts in this book. Steve Tarpinian spent five years developing this video, and the reviews from coaches and athletes agree: *Swim Power* will make a major difference in your swimming.

To order *Swim Power*, call 1-800-571-1700 or send check or money order for $39.95 plus $4.99 shipping and handling to:

Total Training Inc.
60 E. Main St., Dept. ES
West Warwick, RI 02893

For information regarding swim clinics and multisport workshops write to:

Total Training Inc.
78 New Hyde Park Rd.
Franklin Square, NY 11010
or call 1-800-469-2538

INDEX